# Cheating God

# Cheating God

## Malachi:
## A Summons to Holy Service

*Newton C. Conant*

**CHRISTIAN LITERATURE CRUSADE**
Fort Washington, Pennsylvania 19034

**CHRISTIAN LITERATURE CRUSADE**
Fort Washington, Pennsylvania 19034

**CANADA**
Box 189, Elgin, Ontario KOG 1EO

**GREAT BRITAIN**
51 The Dean, Alresford, Hants., SO24 9BJ

**AUSTRALIA**
P. O. Box 91, Pennant Hills, N.S.W. 2120

**NEW ZEALAND**
591 Dominion Road, Auckland 3


Copyright © 1985
Newton C. Conant
This First Printing 1985

*ISBN 0-87508-146-0*

All Rights Reserved. No part of this publication may be translated, reproduced, or transmitted in any form or by any means, electronic or mechanical, including photocopy, recording, or any information storage and retrieval system, without permission in writing from the publisher.

Scripture quotations are from *The New Scofield Reference Bible*. Copyright © 1967 by Oxford University Press, Inc.

PRINTED IN THE UNITED STATES OF AMERICA

## *Contents*

| | |
|---|---|
| Foreword | vii |
| Introduction | ix |
| 1 Controversies With God | 1 |
| 2 In What Way Hast Thou Loved Us? | 7 |
| 3 In What Way Have We Despised Thy Name? | 21 |
| 4 The Priesthood—Cursed or Blessed? | 31 |
| 5 God's Standards for His Priests | 37 |
| 6 Sins Against the Family | 49 |
| 7 Where Is the God of Justice? | 63 |
| 8 How Have We Robbed Thee? | 75 |
| 9 The Precious God-Fearers | 85 |
| 10 The Terrible, Glorious Day of the Lord | 91 |
| 11 Conclusion | 99 |

## *Appreciation*

I deeply appreciate the excellent editing of the manuscript by Mr. Robert Delancy of the Christian Literature Crusade staff.

## *Foreword*

Pastor Newton C. Conant writes not simply after hours in the study but after years of ministering the Word of God to human hearts. Some thirty years ago it was my privilege to be on the receiving end of his prayerful exposition of the book of Malachi. As is God's wonderful way, He providentially put in the same room a man fully equipped to teach His Word and a teenage heart in desperate need to hear it.

At that time in my life I was making some life-shaping decisions out of despair rather than faith. I knew the Lord, but like the people addressed by the prophet Malachi I was cheating God of what rightfully belonged to Him. I had attended many meetings as a staff member at Harvey Cedars Bible Conference, but Pastor Conant's series of messages on Malachi was very special. The Lord used His servant to emphasize the very things I needed to hear. The course of my life was changed as despair gave way to a renewed faith.

It is encouraging to see Pastor Conant's thoughts on Malachi preserved in print for the benefit of many. The message of Malachi is very much needed in our time. We have seen an evangelical groundswell in the United States, but American Christianity is infected with the same spiritual disease that was evident in Israel in Malachi's day. A reading of Newton Conant's work will help you to understand both the problem and its answer.

Dr. John E. Grauley, Director
The Middle Georgia Pastoral Counseling Center, Macon, Georgia; also Associate Professor of Practical Theology, Biblical Theological Seminary, Hatfield, Pennsylvania.

# *Introduction*

*God needs men.* Men who will submit to His crushing discipline. Men anointed with the Holy Spirit. God's work in the world moves ahead as God finds these men. The history of each great movement of the power of God is largely the record of a man God could use, like Moses, Joshua, Martin Luther, Adoniram Judson, Hudson Taylor and D. L. Moody. God searches for such men. "For the eyes of the Lord run to and fro throughout the whole earth, to show himself strong in the behalf of them whose heart is perfect toward him" (II Chronicles 16:9). "And I sought for a man among them, that should make up the hedge, and stand in the gap before me for the land, that I should not destroy it; but I found none" (Ezekiel 22:30).

It was written of Robert M. McCheyne that "to know him was the best interpretation of many texts. . . . His preaching was a continuation of his prayers. He spoke from within the veil."

Malachi writes during a time of sad spiritual declension in Israel. The failure of God's work in that day was the record largely of the failure of God's ministers, the priests. God cannot fail; His servants, however, may.

Malachi's exact date is not known. It is generally accepted that he lived nearly 100 years after Haggai and Zechariah; and that he was associated with Ezra and Nehemiah in their reforms. His date is placed approximately at 450-400 B.C.

A remnant had returned from Captivity (536 B.C). Under the leadership of Haggai and Zechariah they had rebuilt the Temple (520-516 B.C.). Then 60 years later (457 B.C.), Ezra came to help reestablish the nation. Then, 13 years later (444 B.C.), Nehemiah came and rebuilt the wall.

Thus, in Malachi's time, the Jews had been home from Babylon about 100 years, cured, by the Captivity, of their idolatry, but prone to neglect the House of God. The priests had become lax and degenerate. Sacrifices were inferior. Tithes were neglected. The people had reverted to their old practice of intermarrying with idolatrous neighbors (*Halley's Bible Handbook, New Revised Edition,* p. 384).

The religious outburst which immediately followed the return from Babylon had severely declined. The priests and the people they led had fallen into deep spiritual corruption.

God still speaks today through the inspired book of Malachi to point out pitfalls to disaster as well as blessed pathways to fruitfulness to all those who are called to minister in His name.

This book of Malachi, recording as it does the ministry of those called to serve God, necessarily contains many basic principles teaching us all how to obtain the blessing of God and how to avoid failure, frustration, and barrenness. Many of God's servants, it is believed, need to be led forth into a life of victorious, restful, fruitful, Christ-honoring ministry. This book is written with these dear servants of God in mind. This book is, therefore, an honest effort to perform a duty laid upon me: to humbly pass on to God's dear servants who follow, lessons learned in the school of Christ in over sixty years of precious, privileged service.

May God find us to be "vessels unto honor, sanctified and fit for the Master's use, and prepared unto every good work" (II Timothy 2:21).

What a blessed, holy joy to be disciplined by God and to be anointed by the Holy Spirit to serve Him.

Newton C. Conant

**Chapter 1**

# *Controversies With God*

*"O man, who art thou that repliest against God?"* (Romans 9:20).

God has a holy concern for the lives and ministry of all who are called to serve Him. He must have clean, disciplined servants. "Be ye clean, that bear the vessels of the Lord" (Isaiah 52:11). So God in great faithfulness and with complete knowledge pointed out to the priests of that day the areas in which they were in conflict with Him. Instead of readily accepting God's correct analysis and confessing their errors, these priests disputed God's testimony and entered into controversy with Him.

Let me indicate these various controversies with God:

1. I have loved you, saith the Lord.

   *Yet ye say, In what way hast thou loved us?* (1:2).

2. If I be a father, where is mine honor? And if I be a master, where is my fear? saith the Lord of hosts unto you, O priests, that despise my name.

   *And ye say, In what way have we despised*

1

*thy name?* (1:6).

3. Ye offer polluted bread upon mine altar.

*And ye say, In what way have we polluted thee?* (1:7).

4. And if ye offer the blind for sacrifice, is it not evil? And if ye offer the lame and the sick, is it not evil? Should I accept this of your hand? saith the Lord.

*Yet ye say, Why?* (1:8,13; 2:14).

5. Ye have wearied the Lord with your words.

*Yet ye say, In what way have we wearied him?* (2:17).

6. Return unto me, and I will return unto you, saith the Lord of hosts.

*But ye said, In what way shall we return?* (3:7).

7. Will a man rob God? Yet ye have robbed me.

*But ye say, How have we robbed thee?* (3:8).

8. Your words have been stout against me, saith the Lord.

*Yet ye say, What have we spoken so much against thee?* (3:13).

9. God promises great blessing to all who obey Him.

*Ye have said, It is vain to serve God; and what profit is it?* (3:10-12,14).

In addition to all of the controversies enumerated above, many of these priests had put away the wives of their youth and married heathen wives (2:11,14).

How frightful to be attempting to minister in the things of God while being in rebellion against Him! Does not such controversy reveal:

    1. Loss of reverence for the holiness of God.
    2. Loss of the sense of the high calling of the priesthood.
    3. Loss of respect for and obedience to the Word of God.
    4. Priests who, while pretending to serve God, are no longer walking with Him (Amos 3:3), and therefore are totally unfit to reveal the heart and mind of God to the people whom they are called to serve.

How easily forgotten by Malachi's generation were the vows of the remnant who had been in captivity in Babylon. They had said, "If I forget thee, O Jerusalem, let my right hand forget her cunning. If I do not remember thee, let my tongue cleave to the roof of my mouth; if I prefer not Jerusalem above my chief joy" (Psalm 137:5-6). Their hearts had thrilled with the prospect of communion with God someday in a rebuilt temple. How easy for Malachi's generation to forget these sacred hopes and vows. How appropriate the words of Psalm 106:12-13: "Then believed they his words; they sang his praise. They soon forgot his works; they waited not for his counsel."

Where would God's servants be if it were not for God's constant chastening, refining and cleansing! To the priests "He exhibits the worm and decay which lay under falsely whited exteriors" (Pusey, *Minor Prophets*).

God's great desire for His servants is that they increasingly grow in a knowledge of Him and likewise in the knowledge of themselves.

"Grow in grace, and in the knowledge of our Lord and Savior Jesus Christ" (II Peter 3:18).

"I have heard of thee by the hearing of the ear, but now mine eye seeth thee. Wherefore I abhor myself, and repent in dust and ashes" (Job 42:5-6).

Disaster will always be the portion of all who rebel in controversy against God. God's servants are not spared this judgment. King Uzziah was a godly king. "And he sought God in the days of Zechariah, who had understanding in the visions of God; and as long as he sought the Lord, God made him to prosper" (II Chronicles 26:5). "But when he was strong, his heart was lifted up to his destruction; for he transgressed against the Lord his God, and went into the temple of the Lord to burn incense upon the altar of incense" (II Chronicles 26:16). Despite the protest of Azariah the priest and eighty other priests of the Lord, Uzziah in pride and anger refused to turn back and was smitten with leprosy, and later died in an isolated house. Disaster always follows even a child of God who enters into controversy with God and who refuses to yield to God.

After a missionary message during a Missionary Conference, the writer was greeting people as they left the church. One woman said, "I was called to be a missionary. But I turned back and married against God's will." What disaster followed! She had been brutally mistreated; her husband finally was sent to a mental institution. But this isn't all. Think of the blessing those on the mission field did not get, and also the glory which did not come to God. One thing which stands out in the memory of the wedding ceremony of this couple is the solo which was sung. The bride's sister sang "Saviour, Like a Shepherd Lead Us." So much like the condition of the priests of whom Malachi writes. Lip service to God while persisting in rebellion against Him!

God's servants have been known to rebel against His wise choice as to where they are to serve. Others have fought God and persisted in an unholy friendship and later unscriptural marriage. Whatever the area of rebellion, the end is always disaster to the man or woman of God, besides loss of fruitfulness and loss of glory due the name of God.

O servants of the living God, may there not be even the slightest controversy with God in any area of our lives, but a glad and holy surrender to the One who only seeks our highest good and greatest fruitfulness, for His glory.

**Chapter 2**

# *In What Way Hast Thou Loved Us?*

*"I have loved you, saith the Lord. Yet ye say, In what way hast thou loved us?"* (1:2)

The recurring testimony of God's Word is, "I have loved thee and still do love thee with a gracious and everlasting love." God's dealing with Israel is one long record of constant, unfailing love: "The Lord had a delight in thy fathers to love them, and he chose their seed after them, even you above all people, as it is this day" (Deuteronomy 10:15). "Yea, I have loved thee with an everlasting love; therefore, with loving-kindness have I drawn thee" (Jeremiah 31:3). "And because he loved thy fathers, therefore he chose their seed after them, and brought thee out in his sight with his mighty power out of Egypt" (Deuteronomy 4:37). "The Lord did not set his love upon you, nor choose you, because ye were more in number than any people; for ye were the fewest of all people. But because the Lord loved you, and because he would keep the oath which he had sworn unto your fathers, hath the Lord brought you out with a mighty hand, and redeemed you out of the house of bondage, from the hand of Pharaoh, King of Egypt" (Deuteronomy 7:7-8).

The solemn oath which God made first to Abraham (Genesis 12:1-3), and later repeated to Isaac (Genesis 26:3-5), and then to Jacob (Genesis 28:13-15), was a mark of His great love for Israel. This oath included the assurance that Israel would become a great nation through whom eventually all families of the earth would be blessed by the promised Messiah, the Lord Jesus Christ.

God, in great patience, replies to Israel's unkind and false accusation that He did not love them. He needs to point out just one fact of history. *"Was not Esau Jacob's brother? saith the Lord; yet I loved Jacob and I hated Esau"* (1:2). Then God calls attention to Edom's perpetual destruction as a nation in contrast to Israel's preservation and promised future glory. *"I hated Esau, and laid his mountains and his heritage waste for the jackals of the wilderness"* (1:3). Yes, in spite of God's frequent chastisement of the Israelites for their sins, their very preservation is evidence of His sovereign love for Israel in preference to Edom.

But Edom and Israel were *equally guilty* before God. Israel had even more of God's light than Edom. Except for the sovereign will of God, both Edom and Israel should have been left to perish as nations. So Israel's survival after the Exile is clear evidence of God's love and grace; while Edom's destruction is a mark of God's righteous judgment.

It may be asked, Why did Israel question God's

## IN WHAT WAY HAST THOU LOVED US?

love? Israel was in a very poor condition materially compared to the past splendor and luxury of Solomon's reign. Even in the time just before the Exile, when the magnificent temple was still standing, they were far better off materially than now. Their present, rather poor conditions were the direct result of past disobedience to God — of refusing to heed the warning given by prophets sent to Israel. We read: "And the Lord God of their fathers sent to them by his messengers, rising up early and sending, because he had compassion on his people, and on his dwelling place. But they mocked the messengers of God, and despised his words, and misused his prophets, until the wrath of the Lord arose against his people, till there was no remedy. Therefore, he brought upon them the king of the Chaldeans, who slew their young men with the sword in the house of their sanctuary, and had no compassion upon young man or maiden, old man, or him who stooped for age; he gave all into his hand. And all the vessels of the house of God, great and small, and the treasures of the king, and of his princes; all these he brought to Babylon. And they burned the house of God, and broke down the wall of Jerusalem, and burned all its palaces with fire, and destroyed all its precious vessels. And those who had escaped from the sword carried he away to Babylon, where they were servants to him and his sons until the reign of the kingdom of Persia" (II Chronicles 36:15-20).

God will not protect His people in their rebellion. When Israel left God, Israel left her Protector ... with His blessing materially as well as spiritually. How greatly the magnificent temple of Solomon exceeded the present, rather poor temple built by the returning remnant. "Who is left among you that saw this house in its first glory? And how do ye see it now? Is it not in your eyes in comparison with it as nothing?" (Haggai 2:3). "The old men who had seen the first house, when the foundation of this house was laid before their eyes, wept with a loud voice" (Ezra 3:12). God, however, assures this remnant that even with a temple of lesser splendor they have Him — and after all, He is greater than any temple. "Be strong, all ye people of the land, saith the Lord, and work; for I am with you, saith the Lord of hosts" (Haggai 2:4). It is as if God is saying, "I am all you need; do not fret because of a modest temple. *You have me!*"

Israel at this time is an illustration of ingratitude, ignoring all the past and present mercies of God in light of their poorer circumstances due to the sins of their forefathers.

How frightening to consider the complaints of the people and especially the ministry of the priests, who were going through the outward performance of serving God while at the same time questioning His love.

Esau and Jacob were equally related to Abraham (Genesis 25:24-26). Yet God now declares, *"I loved Jacob and I hated Esau"* (1:2-3). God is sovereign; but His sovereignty here is not spoken of as reprobating anyone. No, that is not the meaning of these words. Rather, what seems to be in view is the survival of the nation of Israel — clearly due to God's grace — while the nation of Edom is allowed to perish in just destruction.

God's love is shown in *preferring* Jacob to Esau. In comparing the above with two statements by our Lord Jesus Christ, it may be seen that *love* and *hatred* are at times used to express preference. Jesus said: "If any man come to me, and *hate* not his father, and mother, and wife, and children, and brethren and sisters, yea, and his own life also, he cannot be my disciple" (Luke 14:26). Surely God would not through His Son lead us to disobey Exodus 20:12, where we are commanded to *love* father and mother. The passage in Matthew 10:37 makes it perfectly plain that we are to love our Lord Jesus Christ *more than* anyone in our family: "He that loveth father or mother more than me is not worthy of me; and he that loveth son or daughter more than me is not worthy of me."

It may be fitting also to consider the constant hatred of Esau toward Jacob. Throughout the centuries, Edom had been the cruel enemy of God's people Israel. Thus Esau through his descendants was opposed to all that God in His sovereignty purposed to accomplish through Israel. *This fact alone* justifies God's judgment upon Edom. We first see the hatred exhibited by the Edomites when Israel, recently delivered from the bondage in Egypt, was journeying through the wilderness:

"Moses sent messengers from Kadesh unto the king of Edom. Thus saith thy brother Israel, Thou knowest all the travail that hath befallen us; how our fathers went down into Egypt, and we have dwelt in Egypt a long time; and the Egyptians vexed us and our fathers; and when we cried unto the Lord, he heard our voice, and sent an angel, and hath brought us forth out of Egypt: and, behold, we are in Kadesh, a city in the uttermost of thy border. Let us pass, I pray thee, through thy country. We will not pass through the fields, or through the vineyards, neither will we drink of the water of the wells: we will go by the king's highway, we will not turn to the right hand nor to the left, until we have passed thy borders.

"And Edom said unto him, Thou shalt not pass by me, lest I come out against thee with the sword.

"And the children of Israel said unto him, We will go by the highway; and if I and my cattle drink of thy water, then I will pay for it: I will only, without doing anything else, go through on my feet.

"And he said, Thou shalt not go through. And Edom came out against him with many people, and with a strong hand" (Numbers 20:14-20).

It was a tender plea of a needy brother to a brother who could help. A plea by those who had been delivered by an angel of God from years of hard bondage in Egypt, who merely asked to pass through Edom's territory and who would cause no loss to Edom as they passed through. Their earnest

## IN WHAT WAY HAST THOU LOVED US?    13

plea was met with a bitter refusal, with the threatening of the sword!

The prophets later spoke of the certain judgment due to the people of Edom because of their determined hatred of Israel. "For this violence against thy brother, Jacob, shame shall cover thee, and thou shalt be cut off forever. In the day that thou stoodest on the other side, in the day that the strangers carried away captive his forces, and foreigners entered into his gates and cast lots upon Jerusalem, even thou wast one of them. But thou shouldest not have looked on the day of thy brother in the day that he became a stranger; neither shouldest thou have rejoiced over the children of Judah in the day of their destruction; neither shouldest thou have spoken proudly in the day of distress" (Obadiah 10-12). God speaks also of Edom having "laid hands on their substance in the day of their calamity" (Obadiah 13). The result: "Edom shall be a desolate wilderness for the violence against the children of Judah, because they have shed innocent blood in their land" (Joel 3:19).

Psalm 137:7 apparently contains the record of the attitude of Edom to Judah when Nebuchadnezzar was destroying Jerusalem, and with it Solomon's temple. "Remember, O Lord, the children of Edom in the day of Jerusalem; who said, Raze it, raze it, even to the foundation thereof." When Nebuchadnezzar advanced against Israel the Edomites had gladly welcomed the opportunity for revenge, and joining his forces, exultingly bore their part in the degradation and ruin of their ancient foe. The Edomites shouted, "Down with it, down with it even to the ground" — and they even stood in the passes to intercept any from Jerusalem who attempted to escape.

"Thus saith the Lord God: Because Edom hath dealt against the house of Judah by taking vengeance, and hath greatly offended, and revenged himself upon them, therefore, thus saith the Lord God: I will also stretch out mine hand upon Edom" (Ezekiel 25:12-13). "Thus saith the Lord: for three transgressions of Edom, and for four, I will not turn away its punishment, because he did pursue his brother with the sword, and did cast off all pity, and his anger did tear perpetually, and he kept his wrath forever" (Amos 1:11).

I have felt led to go into some detail to make clear God's righteous pronouncement of judgment upon Edom. Edom, however, was fully determined to thwart God's sentence of total destruction. *"We are impoverished, but we will return and build the desolate places,"* they boasted (1:4). God therefore declares that all their efforts to again rebuild will come to nothing: *"They shall build, but I will throw down."* Edom will be called, says the prophet, *"The border [country] of wickedness, and, The people against whom the Lord hath indignation forever"* (1:4). Edom will be blotted out forever, in contrast to Israel's glorious future. *"The Lord will be magnified from the border of Israel"* (1:5).

In the light of their current difficulties, those

who had returned from the Exile ignored or forgot God's wonderful past dealings with the nation. Israel had lost sight of its history with God. Israel had experienced over 1400 years of God's faithfulness, yet apparently had forgotten God's personal dealings with Abraham, Isaac and Jacob, plus the marvelous preservation of the nation in Egypt by means of Joseph and later the deliverance under Moses. They were not recalling God's tender care during the wilderness journey, and the miracle power displayed through the leadership of Joshua in Canaan. The glorious peak the nation had reached under Solomon was ignored. Both before the Captivity and during the Exile, God had raised up faithful prophets who ministered the word of God to His people. Not only was Israel ignoring her wonderful history with God, she apparently was unconcerned and had ceased to believe in the fulfillment of the glorious promise recorded in Isaiah 2 and Micah 4. "And it shall come to pass in the last days, that the mountain of the Lord's house shall be established in the top of the mountains, and shall be exalted above the hills; and all nations shall flow unto it. And many people shall go and say, Come ye, and let us go up to the mountain of the Lord, to the house of the God of Jacob; and he will teach us of his ways, and we will walk in his paths; for out of Zion shall go forth the law, and the word of the Lord from Jerusalem. And he shall judge among the nations, and shall rebuke many peoples; and they shall beat their swords into plowshares, and their spears into pruning hooks; nation shall not lift up sword against nation, neither shall they learn war any more" (Isaiah 2:2-4).

Is not this the burden of Stephen's message to the Sanhedrin, recorded in Acts 7? Israel had forgotten her history with God! Stephen skillfully traces it for them, and pointedly makes a present application, citing God's faithfulness to the nation and the nation's rejection of Him. "Ye stiff-necked and uncircumcised in heart and ears, ye do always resist the Holy Spirit; as your fathers did, so do ye" (Acts 7:51).

Is it not also rather easy for us who are called to be God's messengers today to forget all of God's past mercies and personal love in the light of a present trial, chastening or difficulty which may be extremely painful to us? (We may or may not have been the cause of the suffering which God has allowed.)

God wants us to remember our history with Him. "And thou shalt remember all the way which the Lord thy God led thee these forty years in the wilderness, to humble thee, and to test thee, to know what was in thine heart, . . . that He might make thee know that man doth not live by bread only, but by every word that proceedeth out of the mouth of the Lord doth man live" (Deuteronomy 8:2-3). As for Israel, so for us. God wants us to see clearly and to remember that the purpose of all His dealings with us is to bring us to the end of all our

## IN WHAT WAY HAST THOU LOVED US?  17

human resources and into more and more complete dependence upon Him, recognizing our helplessness. It is vital to our spiritual lives that we remember God's dealings with us. Let us not forget the history of God's past faithfulness to us in the light of a present difficulty or trial.

I have found it extremely helpful to keep a record of God's gracious leadings in my life and to occasionally review them, especially in times of suffering or trial. Strength and assurance to face the future comes by knowing that God, who has been so faithful in years past, will be all that is needed in the current circumstances.

I was greatly privileged, honored, and blessed by God to be sent by Him to Kenya, Africa, as a missionary at age 70; but the experience was not without its trials — trials that could crush a person. The loneliness, the culture shock, personality conflicts, heavy teaching responsibilities — all could lead to despair. How strengthening at such times to "remember all the way which the Lord thy God led thee." Instead of questioning God's love, we are led more deeply than ever to realize this love in an utterly new way, and to know that there can never come a circumstance that can separate us from the active, participating love of God (Romans 8:35-39).

Shortly after arrival at the mission station in Kenya, my heart seemed completely overwhelmed. My extreme loneliness was largely due to the recent death of my beloved wife of many years. Our comfortable, modest home was missed; it seemed very difficult to go on. At this time God recalled to my mind His gracious dealings in trials in times past, when John 12:24 was found to be the way of joyous deliverance. Once more this lesson had to be learned — in still deeper personal death to self. "Except a grain of wheat fall into the ground and die, it abideth alone; but if it die, it bringeth forth much fruit." The prayer followed: "Lord, make me that grain of wheat now. I am willing." God's peace flooded my heart. The surroundings now glowed with His presence; and blessed and fruitful years followed. F. B. Meyer, whose writings have been such a blessing to me and under whose ministry I once sat, has beautifully written: "Loneliness, solitude, temptation, conflict — these are the flames that burn the divine colours into the character; such the processes through which the blessings of our anointing are made available for the poor, the broken-hearted, the prisoners, the captives, and the blind" (*David: Shepherd, Psalmist, King,* p. 161).

How blessed to recall our past history of the faithfulness of God to us — in times of trial!

I received an earnest request several years ago to visit a pastor's wife who was going through a crushing trial, causing her severe emotional problems. This pastor's wife had a brother whom she dearly loved who was also a pastor, and who was cruelly murdered by a man who supposedly had come for counseling. She felt that perhaps an older, experienced pastor, to whom she might speak at length concerning her spiritual needs, could give words of comfort and assurance. Her husband was most sympathetic. What scriptural comfort could one give at such a time? After quietly looking to God for guidance, the Holy Spirit led me to meditate upon the martyrdom of James.

The Apostle John had a brother James, whom he dearly loved, for he was very close to him. His brother was, Scripture tells us, cruelly murdered (Acts 12:2). However, this severe trial did not shake John's belief in God's unfailing love. He wrote later: "And we have known and believed the love that God hath to us" (I John 4:16). These words of John I meditated upon, and then I trusted the Holy Spirit to apply them to the heart of His needy child, teaching her that in the midst of her most severe trial she was to believe in God's unfailing love . . . even though she might not be able in her mind to reconcile God's love with her present extreme suffering.

It has been well said that "It is only in this life that we have the opportunity to trust God in the dark." There will be no such opportunity in Glory. Failure on the part of a servant of God to believe in His love could destroy an effective, fruitful ministry. A young pastor once remarked to me, "I cannot speak at my prayer meeting tonight. I am seeking a replacement. I am so upset and worried about problems in the church that I am in no condition to speak." Was not God denied the opportunity to demonstrate once more His glorious provision? What of those challenging words, "Nay, in all these things we are more than conquerors through him that loved us" (Romans 8:37)?

Dear servants of God and companions in tribulation, let us believe and rest in the love that God has manifested to us.

## Chapter 3

# *In What Way Have We Despised Thy Name?*

*"A son honoreth his father, and a servant his master; if, then, I be a father, where is mine honor? And if I be a master, where is my fear? saith the Lord of hosts unto you, O priests, that despise my name. And ye say, In what way have we despised thy name?"* (1:6).

The name of our Lord is mentioned so very prominently in Malachi, there being at least thirty-four references to His glorious name. The expression "Lord of Hosts" is mentioned twenty-four times. The name of our Lord includes all that He is: the sum of all His glorious attributes. He is holiness, wisdom, power, light, love. All that God is, He purposes to be on behalf of His redeemed people. God stands absolutely alone. He asks, "To whom, then, will ye liken me?" (Isaiah 40:25). "I am the Lord, and there is none else, there is no God beside me" (Isaiah 45:5). "I have sworn by myself, the word is gone out of my mouth in righteousness and shall not return, that unto me every knee shall bow, and every tongue shall swear" (Isaiah 45:23). The name which some day will be universally honored by all in heaven, in earth, and under the earth was being greatly dishonored by the priests who were called to serve Him.

God in great patience and tenderness answers their rather impudent question *"In what way have we despised thy name?"* He is so faithful to indicate the point of departure from His will. What utter ruin would be the portion of many of God's children if it were not for the faithfulness of God in revealing to us our sins. How necessary the purging and the chastening. What a mark of His constant love (Hebrews 12:4-13)!

God points to the altar. There the erring priests will get God's answer if they have spiritual ears with which to hear and spiritual eyes with which to see and understand. *"Ye offer polluted bread upon mine altar"* (1:7).

The Lord here speaks of the inferior offerings that have been placed on His altar. "Polluted bread" could be better translated as "defiled food" — referring not to the daily showbread but unquestionably to the unfit animals being offered for sacrifice, as is made clear in the next verse. (The New King James Version, the New American Standard Version, the New English Bible and the New International Version unitedly translate this as "defiled food.")

God's charge seems to shock the priests. They reply, *"In what way have we polluted [defiled] thee?"* (1:7). And so the Lord elaborates. But before pointing to the specific evidence — their improper offerings — He refers to their inner attitude of contempt: *"In that ye say, The table of the Lord is contemptible"* (1:7). It is from this that their sinful actions have sprung.

The law which was available to the priests, and which they should have been observing, gave detailed instructions about what should be offered to God and what should not be offered. "He shall offer it *without blemish* before the Lord" (Leviticus 3:1). "Ye shall offer at your own will a male *without blemish.* . . . But whatsoever hath a blemish, that shall ye *not* offer; for it shall not be acceptable for you. . . . It shall be perfect to be accepted; there shall be *no blemish* therein. Blind, or broken, or maimed, or having a wen, or scurvy, or scabbed, ye shall *not* offer these unto the Lord" (Leviticus 22:19-22). Look at the altar! What is on it? *"If ye offer the blind for sacrifice, is it not evil? And if ye offer the lame and the sick, is it not evil?"* (1:8). In direct disobedience to the Word of God, in avarice and greed, the people and priests kept the best of the flock for themselves. They offered to God that which could not be sold or eaten.

The priests were offering to God upon the altar that which was practically worthless, and which therefore had cost the offerer nothing. In contrast, how noble the reply of King David to Araunah. Araunah had offered to *give* David his threshing floor as a place to erect an altar to God. David refused the generous offer with these words, "Nay, but I will surely buy it of thee at a price; neither will

I offer burnt offerings unto the Lord my God of that which cost me nothing" (II Samuel 24:24).

Shall the glorious privilege of serving our Lord cost His servants nothing? "So likewise, whosoever he is of you that forsaketh not all that he hath, cannot be my disciple" (Luke 14:33).

Is not our Lord worthy of the best? I recall ministering one time in a church retirement home. The radio there became useless and the matron remarked, "Let us buy a new one quick, before some church brings in an old radio that nobody wants." Missionaries deeply appreciate the sacrificial love behind many gifts reaching the field, but occasionally one has to smile at the contents of a missionary barrel arriving on the field from home. Some items are so antiquated as to not be worth the freight it took to get them there.

Another serious matter is the nature of the plan of God: that these offerings were to illustrate the one supreme offering of the Lamb of God on the altar of the cross. How could the blind, the lame and the sick properly picture the spotless Lamb of God? "Forasmuch as ye know that ye were not redeemed with corruptible things, like silver and gold, ... but with the precious blood of Christ, as of a lamb *without blemish* and without spot" (I Peter 1:18-19). "Christ . . . offered himself without spot to God" (Hebrews 9:14).

Quite early in Israel's history, as the nation was led out of Egypt, the Passover was instituted with the sacrifice of a lamb "without blemish" (Exodus

12:5). For hundreds of years there was the unbroken testimony that any lamb offered to God must be without defect. The rebellious priests apparently were not exercised about their unscriptural offerings. God therefore reasons with them: When you offer a blind animal for sacrifice, is it not evil? If you were to approach the governor and wanted to gain his favor, would you bring him such an offering and expect him to accept you? Would not this very offering rather show your contempt? The question is, Do you priests have more concern for a human ruler than for the holy God? Is it fitting to offer to God what no one would think of offering to a man of authority (1:8)?

Some years ago there was a police officer in the city of Philadelphia who was held in contempt by some of his fellow policemen. They desired to show their contempt in some way. It was the Christmas season. So they prepared a beautiful gift box and had it presented to this officer by someone he did not know. However, within the box were cinders. The purpose of the "gift" was to relay the message of contempt to this officer from his associates.

Is it not also true that such offerings as the priests were presenting were, in effect, showing contempt for God by defrauding Him of His honor?

*"And now, I pray you, beseech God that he will be gracious unto us"* (1:9). This seems to refer to the priestly blessing recorded in Numbers 6:24-26: "The Lord bless thee, and keep thee; the Lord

make his face shine upon thee, and be gracious unto thee; the Lord lift up his countenance upon thee, and give thee peace." To what avail are such wonderful words, piously uttered, if the one who offers the benediction is showing disrespect to God by his actions. *"This hath been by your means; will he be pleased with thee, or accept thy person?"* (1:9). Or, as the New King James Version so clearly puts it: "While this is being done by your hands, will He accept you favorably?" Of course not! God despises hypocrisy!

*"Who is there even among you that would shut the doors for nothing? Neither do ye kindle fire on mine altar for nothing. I have no pleasure in you"* (1:10). Again we have a translation problem. The New International Version states it plainly: "Oh, that one of you would shut the temple doors, so that you would not light useless fires on my altar! I am not pleased with you." Yes, God despises such offerings. *"I have no pleasure in you, saith the Lord of hosts. Neither will I accept an offering at your hand"* (1:10). "To what purpose is the multitude of your sacrifices unto me? saith the Lord.... Bring no more vain oblations" (Isaiah 1:11,13).

In the midst of the failure of man, God often speaks to us of the time when He will intervene and set His people in order (Psalm 2, Revelation 19). He does so here. He prophecies a time when His perfect will for priests will supplant the present ministry of these and subsequent disobedient priests. It is so good in the time of the failure of

## IN WHAT WAY HAVE WE DESPISED THY NAME?

men to look forward to the time when God, in grace and power, will raise up obedient and fruitful servants who will not fail. His name, now dishonored, will then be glorified. *"For from the rising of the sun even unto the going down of the same, my name shall be great among the nations, and in every place incense shall be offered unto my name, and a pure offering; for my name shall be great among the nations"* (1:11).

God is here predicting the millenial age, when His name — so dishonored by the priests of Malachi's time — will be great, and will be honored by a pure offering.

It is well even today, in the midst of declension and failure, to look away to God's ultimate triumph. We will never be crushed by world conditions if we have read and believed the last three chapters of the Revelation.

God now returns to the subject of the ministry of these rebellious priests. He summarizes the current situation in these plaintive words: *"But ye have profaned it, in that ye say, The table of the Lord is polluted; and the fruit of it, even its food, is contemptible"* (1:12). Then He moves on to another complaint of theirs: *"Ye said also, Behold, what a weariness is it!"* (1:13). How true! What weariness there is in an unconsecrated, unscriptural ministry! God could read their inmost thoughts. The ministry of these priests had become a drudgery to them instead of a keen delight. The service of God should be its own reward; inner delight can be present even when the body is greatly weary. Our Lord Jesus Christ was weary when He sat by Jacob's well. Yet what joy He had when the Samaritan woman received the "well of water springing up into everlasting life" (John 4:1-42). David, in a time of extreme distress, wrote, "Then will I go unto the altar of God, unto God my exceeding joy" (Psalm 43:4).

It is easy to become weary *in* the Lord's work, but one should not become weary *of* it. We never claim it is a weariness to serve a loved one on earth whom we love dearly. This weariness *of* the Lord's work does not proceed from God but rather from an unyielded, rebellious will. "O my people, what have I done unto thee? And in what have I wearied thee? Testify against me" (Micah 6:3).

God further describes their weariness of His calling to the priesthood. *"And ye have sniffed at it, saith the Lord of hosts"* (1:13). Like an animal rejecting food it dislikes — this is the description of the heart attitude of these priests. "Get me out of this monotonous task!" It speaks of repudiation with disgust.

God now pronounces a curse upon the swindling to which these disobedient priests had closed their eyes. *"Cursed be the deceiver who hath in his flock a male, and voweth, and sacrificeth unto the Lord a corrupt thing"* (1:14). A similar curse, mentioned in Deuteronomy 28:58-68, is especially for failure to "fear this glorious and fearful name, The Lord thy God." This name the priests were dishonoring by the corrupt offerings they were permitting offerers to bring to the altar. God's glorious name deserves our complete obedience. *"For I am a great King, saith the Lord of hosts, and my name is terrible among the nations"* (1:14).

May it not be properly said that what the priests really thought of God may be seen in what they placed upon the altar? The believer in the Lord Jesus Christ has been made a priest of God. "Ye are a holy priesthood" (I Peter 2:5). "[He] hath made us a kingdom of priests unto God and his Father" (Revelation 1:6). As priests we have *prescribed spiritual offerings* to "place upon the altar." We are called "to offer up spiritual sacrifices, acceptable to God by Jesus Christ" (I Peter 2:5). These spiritual sacrifices are set forth in Scripture:

1. Our bodies. Romans 12:1 — "I beseech you therefore, brethren, by the mercies of God, that ye present your bodies a living sacrifice, holy, acceptable unto God, which is your reasonable service."

2. Our praise. Hebrews 13:15 — "By him, therefore, let us offer the sacrifice of praise to God continually, that is, the fruit of our lips giving thanks to his name."

3. Our substance. Philippians 4:18 — "I am full, having received of Epaphroditus the things which were sent from you, an odor of a sweet smell, a sacrifice acceptable, well-pleasing to God."

4. Our prayers. Psalm 141:2 — "Let my prayer be set before thee as incense; and the lifting up of my hands as the evening sacrifice."

5. A broken and a contrite spirit. Psalm 51:17 — "The sacrifices of God are a broken spirit; a broken and a contrite heart, O God, thou wilt not despise."

The ultimate purpose of all the offerings is glory to the name of our Lord. "And [he] hath made us a kingdom of priests unto God and his Father; to him be glory and dominion forever and ever. Amen" (Revelation 1:6).

May it not be properly said that what we, as professing Christians, really think about the name of our Lord may be seen by what we have placed on the altar? Have we with joyful hearts desired that these spiritual sacrifices, so sought by our Lord, shall be constantly on the altar? Should we not learn to abhor all attempts of the flesh to intrude? Self-will, pride, desire for recognition, human wisdom, love of praise — these must have no place. This will require our constant vigil and a constant "making-to-die by the Holy Spirit" of all attempts of the flesh to take over.

> Is your all on the altar of sacrifice laid?
> Your heart does the Spirit control?
> You can only be blest and have peace and sweet rest,
> As you yield Him your body and soul.

**Chapter 4**

# *The Priesthood — Cursed or Blessed?*

*"And now, O ye priests, this commandment is for you"* (2:1).

God now speaks directly to His priests. In this section (2:1-9) He declares that there is a path which will lead to unequivocal cursing upon their ministry. And so He clearly reveals what is His standard for the priesthood. In doing this He also points out that a priest who follows His pattern for the priesthood will experience a life of rich fellowship with Him and of blessing to others. Every priest, the Lord makes plain, is either a fountain of evil or a fountain of blessing.

How faithful is God to His servants: He enlightens them to that which if not destroyed will destroy them. He likewise reveals to them what will make them a blessing to others and bring glory to Himself. He purposes greater fruitfulness in their lives. "Every branch that beareth fruit, he purgeth it, that it may bring forth more fruit" (John 15:2).

*"If ye will not hear . . ."* (2:2). Any matter needing correction must be heard with understanding. We are enjoined: "He that hath an ear, let him

hear what the Spirit saith unto the churches" (Revelation 3:13). A dear African student once asked me, "Do you hear Swahili?" The word "hear" to these African students meant to hear effectively — to understand. The result of proper hearing — understanding — will be to "lay it to heart." Twice this expression "lay it to heart" appears in Malachi 2:2.

Heart preparation in the presence of God is the one great necessity for all fruitful ministry. Here God speaks of the opposite situation: *"If ye will not hear, and if ye will not lay it to heart to give glory to my name"* — the name you priests are so dishonoring by your actions — *"I will even send a curse upon you, and I will curse your blessings; yea, I have cursed them already, because ye do not lay it to heart"* (2:2). If these disobedient priests had laid God's word to heart they would never have offered to God that which so clearly violated His law.

Scripture commends Ezra because he had "prepared his heart to seek the law of the Lord, and to do it, and to teach in Israel statutes and ordinances" (Ezra 7:10). In striking contrast, it is written of Rehoboam that "he did evil, because he prepared not his heart to seek the Lord" (II Chronicles 12:14). God now mentions His purpose for all ministry: *"to give glory to my name."* This purpose remains unchangeable forever. Paul declared: "Unto him be glory in the church by Jesus Christ *throughout all ages,* world without end. Amen" (Ephesians 3:21).

## THE PRIESTHOOD — CURSED OR BLESSED? 33

*"I will curse your blessings"* are the awful but necessary warning words of God. All which He has intended to be a source of blessing to these men is about to become a curse. This was no idle threat. The fields which were meant to bring forth abundantly could easily experience the blight of God. God can even organize the destroying insects as instruments of judgment. The statements of earlier prophets had been graphically fulfilled: "That which the palmer worm hath left hath the locust eaten; and that which the locust hath left hath the cankerworm eaten; and that which the cankerworm hath left hath the caterpillar eaten" (Joel 1:4). "Therefore, the heavens over you withhold the dew, and the earth withholds her fruit" (Haggai 1:10).

God gives further warning: *"Behold, I will corrupt your seed"* (2:3). Shall we limit this statement to corruption of seed for planting, or may it not have a wider application also to the seed (children) of the priests? God states later, in Malachi 2:15, that He "seeks a godly seed." This is His purpose in a godly marriage. Eli, the priest of God, failed to live totally for God; his failure certainly produced ungodly seed. The sins of Eli's sons were "very great before the Lord" (I Samuel 2:17). "I will judge his house forever for the iniquity which he knoweth, because his sons made themselves vile, and he restrained them not" (I Samuel 3:12-13).

May it not also be that the ungodly marriages of the priests of Malachi's day made it easier for

Joiada, the son of Eliashib the high priest, to become the son-in-law of Sanballat, who was the constant opponent of God's purpose for His people Israel (Nehemiah 13:28)?

How tragic that the ministry of the priests was about to be overtaken with deserved curses instead of being overtaken with the blessing of God. Moses had declared: "All these blessings shall come on thee, and overtake thee, if thou shalt hearken unto the voice of the Lord thy God.... But it shall come to pass, if thou wilt not hearken unto the voice of the Lord thy God, to observe to do all his commandments and his statutes which I command thee this day, then all these curses shall come upon thee, and overtake thee" (Deuteronomy 28:2,15).

A most serious part of God's curse upon the disobedient priests is now mentioned. It is the total rejection by God of both the offering and its offerer! *"Behold, I will ... spread dung upon your faces, even the dung of your solemn feasts; and one shall take you away with it"* (2:3). Our Lord, when necessary, uses what seems to us to be very strong words describing His needed judgment, as also in Revelation 3:16: "I will spew thee out of my mouth." Here very impressive words are used to show God's holy abhorrence of the despicable offerings which so flagrantly violated His holiness.

God pictures Himself as hurling the dung of the sacrificed animals into the faces of the rebellious priests. Is God not saying that the defective sacrifices the priests were continually offering were as acceptable to Him as dung? *"Behold, I will . . . spread dung upon your faces, even the dung of your solemn feasts."* Not only was the contemptuous offering to be indignantly rejected, but the offerer as well was to be taken away, as worthless, with the offering: *"And one shall take you* [the priests] *away with it."*

How terrible when the priest of God is utterly rejected by God, both as to his ministry and his life, as here. What a glorious contrast as we consider our great high priest Jesus Christ. How perfect the Offering! How holy the Offerer! How beautifully accepted by God!

**Chapter 5**

# *God's Standards for His Priests*

It would be quite unusual if, after revealing the errors of the priests, God did not clearly teach them His righteous standards. God does not only rebuke the disobedient but shows the pathway back to obedience and blessing. The Lord, therefore, speaks of His covenant with Levi (2:4) and then goes into that covenant in detail.

1. *"My covenant was with him of life and peace"* (2:5).

The covenant with the Levitical priesthood contained the fullness of blessing which God had for His people and which was to be ministered through His priests. "Behold, I give unto him my covenant of peace; and he shall have it, and his seed after him, even the covenant of an everlasting priesthood, because he was zealous for his God, and made an atonement for the children of Israel" (Numbers 25:12-13). These words were spoken concerning Phinehas, a grandson of Aaron. Notice that even the *seed* of the obedient priest was to be blessed, in stark contrast to the corrupt seed of the erring priests. "Life and peace" were to flow through the ministry of obedient priests to the needy of Israel. How wonderful that even today "rivers of living water" (John 7:38) flow from God's obedient servants.

2. The Levitical covenant taught awe, fear, respect for the holiness of God (2:5).

*"I gave them* [i.e., life and peace] *to him for the fear with which he feared me, and was afraid before my name"* (2:5). A priest who truly walks with God will experience God's loving chastening and purging, and this will produce the great blessing of being made a "partaker of his holiness" (Hebrews 12:2), resulting in life and peace.

There should ever be an increasing consciousness of the supreme holiness of God, bringing us each to a deeper awareness of our own unworthiness. Even our highest reverence for God is apt to fall far too short. Awe in the presence of the holiness of God is so sadly lacking today in much that is wrongly called worship. How frightful for anyone to attempt to minister in the name of the Lord if he does not have an increasing desire to know and honor the holiness of God. "For thus saith the high and lofty One who inhabiteth eternity, whose name is Holy: I dwell in the high and holy place, with him also who is of a contrite and humble spirit, to revive the spirit of the humble, and to revive the heart of the contrite ones" (Isaiah 57:15).

## GOD'S STANDARDS FOR HIS PRIESTS

3. *"The law of truth was in his mouth"* (2:6).

What a high commendation God gave to Phinehas for his zeal at Baal-peor (Numbers 25). If the words recorded here — "the law of truth was in his mouth" — have a first reference to him, they make him the example of every true priest.

The true priest was to have his heart and mind saturated with the truth of God. Then his mouth would be ready always to speak forth what had been treasured in his heart and mind. There would be a Spirit-filled readiness to apply the truth learned to each needy situation.

Was this not uniquely true of Christ? It is He who is the one speaking through the prophet in Isaiah 50:4: "The Lord God hath given me the tongue of the learned, that I should know how to speak a word in season to him who is weary; he awakeneth [me] morning by morning; he waketh mine ear to hear like the learned." Morning by morning, the Father is seen as awakening His Son from the slumber of the night to teach Him the very words He is to speak that day to the weary ones of earth.

The plea of a busy life cannot be used as an excuse for neglecting heart communion with our Lord Jesus Christ. Joshua, the extremely busy military commander, was commanded: "This book of the law shall not depart out of thy mouth, but thou shalt meditate therein day and night . . . ; for . . . then shalt thou have good success" (Joshua 1:8). A true priest must be a man filled with the Scriptures!

Only then, aided by the Holy Spirit, can the priest reveal the heart and mind of God to the people to whom he is called to minister. Much time must be spent in the presence of the Lord.

4. *"Iniquity was not found in his lips"* (2:6).

The Word of God has a marvelous continuous cleansing power. We are washed by the "water of the word" (Ephesians 5:26). "Now ye are clean through the word which I have spoken unto you" (John 15:3). Constant meditation in the Word will bring "reproof [and] correction [and] instruction in righteousness" (II Timothy 3:16).

It was written of our Lord Jesus Christ that "gracious words proceeded out of his mouth" (Luke 4:22). Psalm 45:2 tells us that grace was poured into His lips. Gracious words, so sorely needed by God's people, will flow forth from the obedient priest as grace flows into him through meditation on the grace and love of God in the Scriptures.

How careful God's ministers should be lest any ungracious, careless words uttered after the sermon should effectively cancel the gracious words spoken from the pulpit. One life in the pulpit; the same life out of the pulpit — the life of Christ, always being manifest in and through the minister!

The life of the minister out of the pulpit should add weight and support to what is preached in the pulpit. It is tragic when the life of a minister seems to say, Don't take too seriously what I have just said in the pulpit. Let us never forget that "*holy* men of God spoke as they were moved by the Holy Spirit" (II Peter 1:21).

5. *"He walked with me in peace and equity"* (2:6).

The true priest walked with God, lived in His presence. His inward peace with God overflowed and manifested itself as peace toward men — in equity, without partiality. This description is a stern rebuke to those priests who "have been partial in the law" (2:9). Paul likewise charges Timothy: "I charge thee before God, and the Lord Jesus Christ, and the elect angels, that thou observe these things without preferring one before another, doing nothing by partiality" (I Timothy 5:21).

Walking with God — walking even like Enoch — implies constant agreement with God in all His judgments. Amos makes it plain that two cannot walk together except they be agreed. It is obvious that the priests of whom Malachi writes were not walking with God, for otherwise there would not have been such a controversy between their actions and God's righteous decrees.

6. *"And did turn many away from iniquity"* (2:6).

The true priest is not satisfied just with his own walk and heart communion with God. He longs that others should turn to God through his ministry and enjoy this same priceless fellowship with God. He has a "turning" ministry. His life and message are a constant call for people to turn to God. God rebukes His ministers who did not stand in His counsel and cause the people to hear His words. "If they had stood in my counsel, and had caused my people to hear my words, then they should have turned them from their evil way, and from the evil of their doings" (Jeremiah 23:22). And He encourages His faithful ministers: "They that be wise shall shine like the brightness of the firmament; and they that turn many to righteousness, as the stars forever and ever" (Daniel 12:3).

The Apostle Paul was called of God to have a "turning" ministry. He was divinely sent "to open their eyes, and to turn them from darkness to light, from the power of Satan unto God" (Acts 26:18). Paul delighted that his ministry was a "turning" ministry. "For they themselves show of us what manner of entering in we had unto you, and how ye turned to God from idols, to serve the living and true God" (I Thessalonians 1:9).

7. *"The priest's lips should keep* [i.e., guard] *knowledge"* (2:7).

The priest should be a guardian of the truth of God committed to him by God. He should be a defender of the faith, one who "earnestly contends for the faith" (Jude 3). "I have kept the faith" was the triumphant confession of the Apostle Paul shortly before his martyrdom (II Timothy 4:7).

God's message is given to His servants as a sacred trust. "But as we were allowed of God to be put in trust with the gospel, even so we speak; not as pleasing men but God, who testeth our hearts" (I Thessalonians 2:4). We are living in a day when often it is difficult to find a church where God's Word in all its purity is preached. The subtle philosophies of men are preached, emphasizing some sort of religion which denies the grace of God. Blind guides lead blind followers into everlasting destruction (Matthew 15:14). Paul exhorted Timothy to "preach the word, ... for the time will come when they will not endure sound doctrine, but, after their own lusts, shall they heap to themselves teachers having itching ears; and they shall turn away their ears from the truth, and shall be turned unto fables. But watch thou in all things, endure afflictions, do the work of an evangelist, make full proof of thy ministry" (II Timothy 4:2-5).

8. *"And they should seek the law at his mouth"* (2:7).

The priest is to have a fruitful counseling ministry. The priest should so live and minister that the people will be encouraged to come to him for help. May the priest be a loving, overflowing fountain, speaking always in full dependence upon God. The people should know where to find help. The priest should be so filled with the Word of God that the Spirit of God can take of the well-digested truth the priest has treasured in his heart and apply it to the needy one who comes for assistance. Only those who are deeply taught by God can truly teach for God. Even as our Lord Jesus Christ was taught by God, so He was enabled to teach for God (John 8:26-28). Unless there is dependence upon God, the best the priest can give the needy inquirer is human, fleshly wisdom, which can never solve problems.

We are living in a day of extreme tension, worry, and perplexity. Conditions at home and abroad which seem to have no solution confront us from every channel of the media. Anxiety cannot help but seep into our minds — and depression is apt to follow. People's hearts are failing them for fear (Luke 21:26). Family problems — with divorce becoming so prevalent — drugs and drunkenness, immorality and violence add to the need for help from God's counselors to His people.

What a privilege and responsibility for God's man! If parsonage walls could speak and relate the heartbroken appeals of those who come to the pastor for help! How necessary for the pastor to seek the mind and heart of God in order to be ready!

I would not pretend to be a counselor to counselors. I wish simply to relate the pathway in which the Lord has seemed to lead me in helping those who come with needs.

Set aside everything else and make the ones coming the most important people in the world to you at that time. Tell the comers how important they are to you now, and assure them that they may have all the time they desire. Often, to relieve uneasiness, cookies and ice cream may be set before them for a time of casual conversation, before the real interview begins (I Kings 19:5-7,

John 21:12-13).

Encourage them to speak first and tell all that is on their minds and hearts. This in itself is a healing therapy. While they are speaking, keep looking to God to bring to your mind appropriate portions of Scripture where at least a little light may be given about the next step to be taken. When this step is taken in faith, more light will be given. This ministry requires self-crucifixion upon the part of the pastor and a joyful willingness to be poured out in order to establish the needy ones in the faith (Philippians 2:17).

How rewarding to the pastor and what glory to God to see souls saved, families kept together, young people consecrated for service, and Christians led out into a life of victory in Christ. How much of Christ's ministry was to individuals! What a counselor He is (Isaiah 9:6, Revelation 3:18)!

9. *"For he is the messenger of the Lord of hosts"* (2:7).

The priest must never forget his high calling as a messenger of the Lord of hosts. He is the mouthpiece for God. There is no higher calling in all the universe, no greater privilege than to speak for God. What a joy and privilege to speak words of life to those dead in sin! "If any man minister, let him do it as of the ability which God giveth, that God in all things may be glorified through Jesus Christ, to whom be praise and dominion forever and ever. Amen" (I Peter 4:11). We read: "Then spoke Haggai, the Lord's messenger, with the

Lord's message unto the people, saying, I am with you, saith the Lord" (Haggai 1:13). How wonderful when the Lord's chosen messenger gives the message of the Lord! "How beautiful are the feet of them that preach the gospel of peace, and bring glad tidings of good things!" (Romans 10:15). "Now, then, we are ambassadors for Christ, as though God did beseech you by us; we beg you in Christ's stead, be ye reconciled to God" (II Corinthians 5:20). What a holy joy to be a messenger bringing the good news of salvation to a world of lost people.

In striking contrast to God's standard for His priests were the priests of Malachi's time. Both in life and ministry they were far from God's ideal.

1. *"But ye are departed out of the way"* (2:8).

The priests had left God's appointed way so clearly outlined for them in the Scriptures and had substituted their own rebellious, unscriptural ministry. God's appointed servants willingly closed their eyes to God's will and then, as always follows, they became hardened and thus insensible to His will (John 12:37-39).

2. *"Ye have caused many to stumble at the law"* (2:8).

Instead of turning people to God, people were turned away from God by the priests. Blinded leaders were misleading blinded followers. "Can the blind lead the blind? Shall they not both fall into the ditch?" (Luke 6:39). "An appalling and horrible thing is committed in the land: the prophets prophesy falsely, and the priests bear rule by their means, and my people love to have it so; and what will ye do in the end of it all?" (Jeremiah 5:30-31).

In our day it is tragic to relate that many people cannot be persuaded to hear the gospel because of the glaring inconsistencies in the life of some pastor.

3. *"Ye have corrupted the covenant of Levi, saith the Lord of hosts"* (2:8).

The covenant of Levi (mentioned in 2:4 through 2:7) was what God ordained for all Levites. But it was being largely ignored and held in contempt. Polluted offerings, ungodly lives, divorcing of wives — what abundant evidence of the corruption of the righteous standards of the covenant of Levi. Therefore life and peace and all the intended blessings which were to follow obedience were forfeited. "Remember them, O my God, because they have defiled the priesthood, and the covenant of the priesthood and of the Levites" (Nehemiah 13:29).

What was God's reaction? *"Therefore have I also made you contemptible and base before all the people, according as ye have not kept my ways, but have been partial in the law"* (2:9).

God made these men contemptible in the eyes of the people to whom they pretended to minister. God made them what they had first made His altar to be by their second-rate offerings: "Ye say, The table of the Lord is contemptible" (1:7).

How sad it is when the minister loses the

respect of those to whom he is sent to minister. How lamentable!

While waiting in the post office, a minister who preceded me in line was telling another joke. He was known for his "off color" remarks. From those who listened a sort of hollow, embarrassed laugh followed. One clerk, who made no profession of following Christ, said to me afterwards, "That man has missed his calling!"

It seems from the context that even those to whom the priests had been partial now turned against the priests in contempt. Yes, even unsaved people can detect the hypocrisy of pastors who favor them for fancied gain, and in heart they hold such pastors in contempt.

## Chapter 6

# *Sins Against the Family*

God now deals with the sinful, immoral lives of the people and priests of Malachi's day (2:10-16). What a horrible combination of sins for these who pretended to worship God and minister for Him! Not only was there iniquity because of the despicable offerings but there was also iniquity in their home life — this is God's testimony regarding His people.

First mentioned are the sins against brotherhood. *"Have we not all one father? Hath not one God created us?"* (2:10). Malachi appeals for unity in the nation and home on the basis of the one father who created Israel. God is the father of His covenant people. "If, then, I be a father, where is mine honor?" (1:6). He is father also in the sense of being the Creator, but He is father in a unique sense to Abraham's descendants.

*"Why do we deal treacherously, every man against his brother, by profaning the covenant of our fathers?"* (2:10). Five times in this short

context the Jews are spoken of as being treacherous (verses 10, 11, 14, 15, 16). The word "treachery" means that a sacred trust has been betrayed. There was the treachery of brother against brother, which was the general result of lightly regarding God's covenant with the nation. But after mentioning this, Malachi moves on quickly to a more specific variety of treachery: treachery in the family itself. The sacred vows of marriage, in which the wife entrusted herself to her husband, had been flagrantly violated. Some men had put away their wives, presumably to marry younger women.

The people were profaning — bringing to nothing, staining with sin — the covenant of their fathers. Before the nation entered Canaan, God had given Israel His warning not to enter into marriages with the people of other nations. "Neither shalt thou make marriages with them; thy daughter thou shalt not give unto his son, nor his daughter shalt thou take unto thy son. For they will turn away thy son from following me, that they may serve other gods; so will the anger of the Lord be kindled against you, and destroy thee suddenly" (Deuteronomy 7:3-4). The identical warning was given to Israel after the new generation occupied Canaan. "If ye do in any way go back, and cling to the remnant of these nations, even these who remain among you, and shall make marriages with them, and go in unto them, and they unto you, know for a certainty that the Lord your God will no more drive out any of these nations from before

## SINS AGAINST THE FAMILY

you; but they shall be snares and traps unto you, and scourges in your sides, and thorns in your eyes, until ye perish from off this good land which the Lord your God hath given you" (Joshua 23:12-13).

*"Judah hath dealt treacherously, and an abomination is committed in Israel and in Jerusalem; for Judah hath profaned the holiness of the Lord which he loved, and hath married the daughter of a foreign god"* (2:11). God speaks of this act as an abomination which profanes His holiness. Marriage is a sacred, holy covenant revealing the holiness of God. Lust, separation, divorcing of wives and marrying heathen wives violates the holiness of God! "And ye shall be holy unto me; for I, the Lord, am holy, and have separated you from other people, that ye should be mine" (Leviticus 20:26). It is impossible for the people to be "holy unto God" while violating His holiness in disregarding the holiness of marriage. Leaving their proper wives, even some of the priests had "married the daughters of a foreign god." How terrible this sin of marrying those who worshiped not Jehovah. What an abundant testimony God had given about avoiding such a sin.

In addition to the many scriptures stressing the importance of separation unto God's will in marriage, there were at least two illustrations which these men ignored which showed the tragedy of marrying heathen wives. Solomon, after teaching about the tremendous peril of lustful, ungodly living, had afterward turned from his own God-inspired proverbs (chapter 5) and married many heathen wives — who so turned his heart from God that he who had built the magnificent temple for God later constructed temples for heathen deities (I Kings 11:1-8). There was also Ahab, the king of Israel who "did evil in the sight of the Lord above all who were before him . . . [in] that he took as his wife Jezebel, the daughter of Ethbaal, king of the Sidonians, and went and served Baal, and worshiped him" (I Kings 16:30-31). Thus was the horrible idolatrous worship of Baal spread throughout Israel. Such examples left these later Israelites without excuse. How these marriages of Solomon and Ahab had violated the holiness of God!

Is it surprising that God speaks of ungodly marriages as uniting the offending layman or priest with the idolatrous worship of the wife: ". . . hath married the daughter of a foreign god"? The ancient rabbis commented: "He who marries a heathen woman is son-in-law to the idol." It was a grave mistake to think that a heathen wife would surely leave her idolatry behind when she married a priest of the Lord. No, false worship comes in with the heathen wife, in one united package.

It seems the priests were marrying into influential families — heathen families established in the land during the Exile — and in that way taking women who were steeped in idolatry. "The people of Israel, and the priests and the Levites, have not separated themselves from the people of the lands, . . . for they have taken of their daughters for themselves, and for their sons, so that the holy seed have mixed themselves with the people of those lands" (Ezra 9:1-2). The priests, who should have been setting a godly example for the rest of the people, were not. How unlike they were to their forefather Phinehas, who with a javelin had abruptly brought to a halt an incident involving intercourse with an ungodly Midianite woman (Numbers 25).

*"The Lord will cut off the man that doeth this, the master and the scholar, out of the tabernacles of Jacob"* (2:12). Master and scholar are words which mean that there will be no exceptions to God's judgment; all classes are included, from the highest to the lowest, whether teacher or student, king or slave.

God is evidently referring to the offerings of the disobedient priests when He speaks specifically of cutting off *"him that offereth an offering unto the Lord of hosts"* (2:12). The context shows that the offerer was being rejected because of his ungodly marriage. "The sacrifice of the wicked is an abomination to the Lord" (Proverbs 15:8). The sacrifices offered by priests who at the same time were turning away from the Word of God were an insult to God, for they implied that God could be bribed.

A very interesting and informative verse follows: *"And this have ye done again, covering the altar of the Lord with tears, with weeping, and with crying out, insomuch that he regardeth not the offering any more, or receiveth it with good will at your hand"* (2:13). Some translators and expositors see these tears as being tears of the priests who wept because their offerings were no longer acceptable. "You weep and wail because he no longer pays attention to your offerings or accepts them with pleasure from your hands" reads the New International Version. If this rendering is accurate, one wonders why evidence of repentance is not seen in amended lives of the priests. Comments by other expositors seem to fit the context better. George Adam Smith writes, "His altar is so wetted by the tears of the wronged women that the gifts offered upon the altar are no longer acceptable in His sight" (*The Book of the Twelve Prophets*, Vol. 2, p. 363). "They by ill treatment occasioned their wives to weep there to God, and God regarded this as though they had stained the altar with their tears. God regarded the tears of the oppressed, but not the sacrifices of the oppressors" (Pusey, *Minor Prophets*, pp. 482-483). It seems only sensible that God who is holy could not accept an offering from a priest so totally indifferent to the holiness of marriage.

*"Yet ye say, Why?"* (2:14). "Why," ask the conscience-hardened priests, "will you not accept our offerings?" The awful brazenness of the hardened heart! God goes into further detail regarding their violation of the holiness of their marriage vows. *"Because the Lord hath been witness between thee and the wife of thy youth, against whom thou hast dealt treacherously; yet is she thy companion,*

*and the wife of thy covenant"* (2:14). How touching these words, "the wife of thy youth." Youth, when newly awakened love was so precious. Youth, when each one joyfully pledged with sacred vows his or her love, tenderness, and care for the other, with never a thought that their precious marriage should ever be anything less than for life. God declares that these priests (and undoubtedly the laymen also) have "dealt treacherously," each one having betrayed the sacred trust of his wife who committed her all to her beloved companion in the sacred covenant of marriage.

How precious is a godly wife to one who ministers. In English mythology there is a story of a wife who sucked the poison out of the wounds which poisoned arrows had inflicted upon her warrior husband in battle. The man of God is a spiritual warrior, called into constant spiritual conflict. The intensity of the battle, with so much depending on victory, will often drain the physical strength . . . and then it is so easy for mental depression to follow. What a joy to have an encouraging word from the dear wife — perhaps with a refreshing treat. Soon the sacred love heals the wounds received in combat.

The heathen wives of these disobedient priests would not *remove* poison but would *pour in more* — the poison of their idolatry. Lust is so cruel, so selfish, so blind to the certain consequences (Galatians 6:8).

One day as I was ministering in a hospital a

woman peered out through the open door of a room and, seeing that I was carrying a Bible, asked me to step in and talk with her and her ill daughter. How pathetic her story, and her appeal for spiritual help: "My husband left me and my daughter for a younger woman. My daughter [who seemed to be in her 20's] needs him so desperately now!" (And she poured out much more.) How common this reason for divorce has become!

*The wife of thy youth, she and she alone* is thy true companion. She alone can fully share the sorrows, the joys, and the burdens of life with you as a true companion. These replacement wives — heathen ones especially — could never be genuine companions in the truest sense. Love did not bring these heathen wives into marriage with the erring priests; *lust* did!

*"And did not he make one? Yet had he the residue of the spirit. And why one? That he might seek a godly seed"* (2:15). Malachi here takes his hearers back to the time when God instituted the family — when He created man and woman and said, "They shall be one flesh" (Genesis 2:24). God made one ideal couple then, a pair designed for each other. Did God stop doing this after He made Adam and Eve? No, He had "the residue of the spirit" — that is, God has an inexhaustible reserve of creative power. His unlimited power enables Him to produce, even today, a vast number of ideally matched couples — godly couples, endued with His Spirit.

"And why one?" Whether referring to Adam and Eve or to later-day couples, God now relates one of the main reasons why He "makes two one." He "seeks a godly seed" — godly children from a godly marriage. For eventually the Messiah would come into the world through a godly line. And the Old Testament priesthood was strictly a hereditary matter, so a godly seed in the priestly line was certainly of vital importance to Israel's religious life.

This "godly seed" principle is forceably brought to the attention of anyone who has been on the mission field. The June 1982 issue of *Fuel for Prayer Fires,* issued by the Africa Inland Mission, asked this question: "Did you know that approximately 100 of A.I.M. missionaries are MK's [missionaries' kids], second and even third generations with the mission? How wonderful to see children and grandchildren of missionaries returning to the mission field." This is as it should be! What a testimony to Christ! I have met many of these second and third generation missionaries. On the other hand, how tragic the words in Ezra 9:1-2: "The people of Israel, and the priests and the Levites, have not separated themselves from the people of the lands.... For they have taken of their daughters for themselves, and for their sons, so that the holy seed have mixed themselves with the people of those lands." How could God's purpose to seek godly children raised in a godly family possibly be realized when the disobedient priests left their God-given wives and took unto themselves heathen wives!

*"Therefore, take heed to your spirit, and let none deal treacherously against the wife of his youth"* (2:15). This is a stirring appeal from God to discern the point of departure — "take heed to your spirit." Twice in this context we find these words. There is always inner corruption before there is an outward fall. Wrong and immoral thoughts, when first suggested to the mind, may seem repulsive. However, if these wrong thoughts are allowed to remain and progress, open sin may follow. It has been well said that "If not resisted, repulsive things become tolerable; then, after becoming tolerable, they become the norm."

There is a battle going on for the mind and spirit of the Christian worker, for the mind and the spirit are the key to all actions. Hence the crucial importance of Paul's words to the morally lax Corinthian church: "Having, therefore, these promises, dearly beloved, let us cleanse ourselves from all filthiness of the flesh and spirit, perfecting holiness in the fear of God" (II Corinthians 7:1).

*"For the Lord, the God of Israel, saith that he hateth putting away"* (2:16). God detests this "putting away" by the priests, and any others, of the wives to whom they had pledged their sacred vows. "I hate divorce" is the straightforward statement here as given in both the New International and the New American Standard versions. Then follows: *"For one covereth violence with his garment, saith*

## SINS AGAINST THE FAMILY

*the Lord of hosts"* (2:16). I believe that this verse refers to an old custom, that of the bridegroom covering his intended wife with his garment. The spread garment over the beloved wife-to-be was a symbol of wedded love and protection. "She is mine! I will be her husband and protector." This is the meaning of Ezekiel 16:8: "Now when I passed by thee, and looked upon thee, behold, thy time was the time of love; and I spread my skirt over thee, and covered thy nakedness. Yea, I swore unto thee, and entered into a covenant with thee, saith the Lord God, and thou becamest mine." God is using the illustration of covering to claim His erring people, Israel, as His very own.

Think also of Ruth, the wife of God's choice for Boaz. She said to him, "I am Ruth, thine handmaid. Spread, therefore, thy skirt over thine handmaid." And Boaz replied, "I will do to thee all that thou requirest; for . . . thou art a virtuous woman." So Boaz took Ruth to be his wife (Ruth 3:9-11).

However, God sees the garment these disobedient priests are casting over the wives of their youth as a garment covering up violence — not symbolizing love and protection: "For one covereth violence with his garment" (2:16).

It may be necessary at this point to sound a much-needed word of warning to pastors and other Christian workers who speak in the name of the Lord. The list of sound, Bible-believing pastors who have fallen through immorality is alarming.

This writer personally knows of at least eight men of God who were overcome by lusts of the flesh and had to leave their places of ministry. It was a terrible experience to be called upon to try to save two of these distraught churches. No doubt these very pastors had spoken vehemently against the very sins which later they allowed to overthrow them. We need only to look at Solomon, who so completely violated his inspired teaching against immorality. How sad!

What a terrible price is paid! The pastor and his family suffer, his ministry is blighted, the church's testimony in the community suffers almost irreparable harm, and above all, God is dishonored.

Heartbreaking incidents can painfully be recalled of the awful price to be paid for immorality. Some years ago a businessman appeared at my parsonage with a sad and bitter story to relate. He had been a prosperous manufacturer, and while attending a convention of fellow business executives he had met a young secretary who persuaded him to leave his wife and family. Now, after a few years, he was a broken man. He said, "I have lost my family, my beautiful home, my business, and I am trying to make a living as a salesman. At the last place I visited I told them part of my plight, and they urged me to come and see you. My new young wife has now left me. I live alone in a room. Please write this up in some form; tell it everywhere as a warning to others." Fortunately he accepted the Lord Jesus Christ as Savior; but oh, the wreck-

## SINS AGAINST THE FAMILY

age that follows immorality!

The first impulse must be resisted. Temptation will come from many sides. A fine pastor with a good family drove his car to the monthly mission service. The pianist had a desire to be taken home last! Undue familiarity developed, and then the awful tragedy affecting the church, family, community, and the glory of God. It happens also on the mission field. A missionary's wife left him to live with a prominent national. The missionary returned home, to the sending church, leaving his wife on the field living in sin. I personally knew a splendid young missionary couple who were commissioned to go to a foreign field . . . where they served for ten years. The saddened wife now walks alone — divorced! Her husband has remarried. The mission field is abandoned.

And so it goes! How we all need to take heed to our spirits with constant resistance of evil, humbling before God, and confession of sin.

Every pastor needs to be especially careful in all relationships with his secretary, who necessarily will spend much time with him. Here a friendship beyond the bounds of propriety could easily develop, with later tragic results. It is well always to pray for guidance and purity before engaging in the necessary work with one's secretary.

How essential for the blessing of the Lord is the godly life of the pastor with his wife. It is only as he learns to live better with his wife that he will preach better. The pulpit is in many ways the extension of the home. It is difficult, if not impossible, to be out of the Spirit in the home and in the Spirit in the pulpit. "In like manner, ye husbands, dwell with them according to knowledge, giving honor unto the wife, as unto the weaker vessel, and as being heirs together of the grace of life, that your prayers be not hindered" (I Peter 3:7). If because of the pastor's wrong living with his wife his prayers are hindered, how can there be any blessing upon his ministry, which depends so much upon answered prayer? It is highly significant that prominently listed among the necessary qualifications of a pastor or elder is his responsibility to maintain a godly home (I Timothy 3:1-5, Titus 1:5-8). Even such often overlooked sins as impatience, irritability, and lack of tenderness in the home will severely cripple one's message from the pulpit.

The words of the Apostle Paul may be an appropriate close to this chapter. "But I keep under my body, and bring it into subjection, lest that by any means, when I have preached to others, I myself should be a castaway" (I Corinthians 9:27) — lest my ministry be disapproved, dishonoring to God and rejected.

**Chapter 7**

# *Where Is the God of Justice?*

*"Where is the God of justice?"* (2:17).

This is the cry of those who question whether there is a God who metes out justice. The implication is that all things are carried along by blind chance; there is no overruling Providence. God is an absentee in His universe. "There are no judgments — look at the wicked who flourish unmolested in their sin! The Babylonians are a fierce, wicked, idolatrous nation; yet they prosper, even having enough gold to overlay a huge image!" (Recall Daniel 3:1.)

Such unbelieving words weary the Lord. *"Ye have wearied the Lord with your words"* (2:17). The Lord was well aware of both their open and secret murmurings. Words which reveal such a total lack of spiritual understanding are tedious to God and repulsive. Especially is this true when the offensive words come from professing believers. We see this well illustrated in the proud boast of the church at Laodicea: "I am rich, and increased with goods, and have need of nothing." But God declares: "Thou art wretched, and miserable, and poor, and blind and naked." This church is called to repent. If there is no repentance, He says, "I will spew thee out of my mouth" (Revelation 3:14-19). The vaunting words of the church at Laodicea which revealed such a total lack of spiritual discernment were abhorrent to God, a terrible weariness to Him.

These Israelites of Malachi's day, instead of accepting God's true estimate of their condition, once more asked God to provide evidence. So the Lord, in great longsuffering and with perfect clarity, quotes their words which weary Him. Some had said, *"Every one that doeth evil is good in the sight of the Lord, and he delighteth in them"*; others had asked, *"Where is the God of justice?"* (2:17).

To these scoffers, God does not seem to have any absolutes as to what is right and what is wrong. If He did, they reason, the wicked would not prosper but would quickly be judged. So evildoers must be guiltless in the sight of the Lord; in fact, He must actually delight in them. For sinners appear to prosper in their iniquity without being judged. "Where is the God of justice? There *is* no discriminating justice!"

How sad that sometimes God's children are tempted to question God's justice as it operates in the present world. If the priests and others of Malachi's time had only meditated on Psalm 73, the problem would have been solved for them as it was for Asaph. "I was envious of the foolish, when I saw the prosperity of the wicked.... And they say, How doth God know? And is there knowledge in the Most High? Behold, these are the ungodly who prosper in the world; they increase in riches.... When I thought to know this, it was too painful for me, until I went into the sanctuary of God; then understood I their end.... How are they brought into desolation, as in a moment!... Whom have I in heaven but thee? And there is none upon earth that I desire beside thee."

God's perfect timing is often a puzzle. When justice seems long delayed, the unbelieving heart is tempted to believe that judgment will never come. However, "the Lord is not slack concerning his promise, as some men count slackness, but is long-suffering toward us, not willing that any should perish, but that all should come to repentance" (II Peter 3:9).

God now gives His answer to the question "Where is the God of justice?" Both the Judge and His justice are now revealed.

*"Behold, I will send my messenger, and he shall prepare the way before me"* (3:1). You priests have failed as true messengers of the Lord. But here is "my messenger," divinely accredited; he will not fail. Who is he? John the Baptist — godly and fearless; he will prepare the way for the God of justice.

Jesus clearly identified John as the explicit fulfillment of this prophecy: "For this is he of whom it is written, Behold I send my messenger before thy face, who shall prepare thy way before thee" (Matthew 11:10). John gave a leveling message of repentance, a message the priests had failed to give. In fact, *they* needed repentance! Isaiah speaks of the message of repentance as one leveling all hearts — like a road is leveled in preparation for the arrival of some great earthly monarch. So repentance is the instrument of leveling which prepares the needy heart to receive the Lord Jesus Christ. "Every valley shall be exalted, and every mountain and hill shall be made low; and the crooked shall be made straight, and the rough places plain" (Isaiah 40:4). Listen to John's fearless preaching: "Repent, for the kingdom of heaven is at hand. . . . I, indeed, baptize you with water unto repentance, but he who cometh after me is mightier than I, whose shoes I am not worthy to bear; he shall baptize you with the Holy Spirit and with fire; whose fan is in his hand, and he will thoroughly purge his floor, and gather his wheat into the granary, but he will burn up the chaff with unquenchable fire" (Matthew 3:2, 11-12). *Here* is the God of justice!

*"The Lord, whom ye seek, shall suddenly come to his temple"* (3:1). How frequently the Scripture gives us both a near and a distant view. "The Lord whom ye seek" I believe to be a distant prophecy. There is no record of Israel as a nation seeking the Lord Jesus Christ during His earthly ministry. Rather, they rejected Him. "Then answered all the people, His blood be on us, and on our children"

(Matthew 27:25). Stephen, in his address before the Sanhedrin, closes with these words about Israel's guilt: "Which of the prophets have not your fathers persecuted? And they have slain them who showed before of the coming of the Just One, of whom ye have been now the betrayers and murderers" (Acts 7:52).

When shall Israel seek our Lord Jesus Christ? It seems clear from Zechariah 12:10-13:1 that this will occur when there is national repentance. The spirit of grace and of supplications will be poured out upon Israel as a nation when it is miraculously delivered from the attempt of the nations under the Beast to destroy it (Zechariah 14:1-3). Looking intently upon the One "whom they have pierced, they shall mourn for him, as one mourneth for his only son, and shall be in bitterness for him, as one that is in bitterness for his firstborn.... In that day there shall be a fountain opened to the house of David and to the inhabitants of Jerusalem for sin and for uncleanness." The Apostle Paul wrote of this day: "And so all Israel shall be saved; as it is written, There shall come out of Zion the Deliverer, and shall turn away ungodliness from Jacob" (Romans 11:26). God hasten the day!

"The Lord . . . shall suddenly come to his temple." The temple, therefore, will be rebuilt. Even though the "man of sin" enters the rebuilt temple and demands worship as God, he will be judged. He will be destroyed with the brightness of our Lord's coming to earth to rule (II Thessalonians 2:3-8). It will be God's temple; the Lord Jesus Christ will be in complete control.

Our Lord is called *"the messenger of the covenant"* (3:1). "I ... will give thee for a covenant of the people, for a light of the nations" (Isaiah 42:6). He is the One who will cause all the covenants to be completely fulfilled. Such covenants as the Abrahamic — a promise to bless all nations through a coming Messiah (Genesis 12:1-3, Isaiah 2:1-4); Israel to inherit a land forever (Genesis 17:7-8); a coming Messiah to occupy the throne of David (Isaiah 9:6-7, Luke 1:31-35); universal peace, with Israel the leading nation of the world (Micah 4:1-5). Our hearts cannot but be concerned as we witness the struggle of Israel now for survival. Former President Jimmy Carter related that in his many interviews with Prime Minister Menachem Begin, Begin constantly referred to Old Testament scriptures as the basis of Israel's right to all the land identified in Joshua 1:3-4. However, the restoration of all this land to Israel awaits the coming of the Messiah in glory to deliver the besieged nation, and the repentance and conversion of the nation. "The zeal of the Lord of hosts will perform this" (Isaiah 9:7).

Israel will then delight in the Lord! *"Whom ye delight in"* (3:1). During the days of His flesh, Israel saw no beauty in Christ that they should desire Him (Isaiah 53:2). However, "Thy people shall be willing in the day of thy power" (Psalm 110:3).

*"Behold, he shall come, saith the Lord of hosts"* (3:1).

The Lord Jesus Christ is now seen as Judge: *"But who may abide the day of his coming? And who shall stand when he appeareth?"* (3:2). Who will prevail in the day of judgment? It is well to recall that all judgment has been given into the hands of our Lord Jesus Christ. "For the Father judgeth no man, but hath committed all judgment unto the Son" (John 5:22). He will judge:

1. The saved — for rewards (II Corinthians 5:10).

2. The harlot church (Revelation 19:2).

3. The Beast and the False Prophet (Revelation 19:20).

4. The gentile nations (Revelation 19:15).

5. The nation of Israel (Zechariah 12:10-13:2).

6. Satan and fallen angels (Revelation 20:10, Jude 6).

7. The unsaved (Revelation 20:15).

How complete His judgments! This should be very comforting to the child of God.

If God is not perplexed by rebellious world conditions, neither would He have His saved ones to be disturbed. The peace that is His will likewise keep us. *He* will write the last triumphant chapter when all will finally be under Christ and the Father (I Corinthians 15:28).

Christ's very presence in judgment is like a refiner's fire. *"For he is like a refiner's fire.... And he shall sit like a refiner and purifier of silver"*

(3:2-3). His very presence is a fire. "Our God is a consuming fire" (Hebrews 12:29). "Every man's work shall be made manifest; for the day shall declare it, because it shall be revealed by fire; and the fire shall test every man's work of what sort it is" (I Corinthians 3:13).

The purging begins with the corrupt priesthood. *"He shall purify the sons of Levi, and purge them like gold and silver, that they may offer unto the Lord an offering in righteousness"* (3:3). Where is the God of justice? We see His judgment beginning with the corrupt priesthood, the very priests who asked this question. There are Levites mentioned in the book of the Acts who were true to the Lord, Barnabas (Acts 4:36) and "a great company of priests" (Acts 6:7). These may be regarded as sort of a first fruit, a pledge of the coming purification of the entire priesthood at the return of Christ in glory. Then they shall *"offer unto the Lord an offering in righteousness. Then shall the offering of Judah and Jerusalem be pleasant unto the Lord, as in the days of old, as in former years"* (3:3-4). Remember how it was at the dedication of the temple: "And it came to pass, when the priests were come out of the holy place, that the cloud filled the house of the Lord, so that the priests could not stand to minister because of the cloud; for the glory of the Lord had filled the house of the Lord" (I Kings 8:10-11). The glory of the Lord filling the house of the Lord was a gracious acknowledgement that the offering was pleasing to the Lord.

Once again, with a purged priesthood, offerings will be made in righteousness as in former years.

Where is the God of justice?

God now enumerates the particular violators of His law who will be dealt with. *"And I will come near to you [in] judgment; and I will be a swift witness against the sorcerers, and against the adulterers, and against false swearers, and against those that oppress the hireling in his wages, the widow, and the fatherless, and that turn aside the sojourner from his right, and fear not me, saith the Lord of hosts"* (3:5).

Is not this last charge, "and fear not me," the real root of all sin? The Apostle Paul gives an extended list of the terrible sins of the human race in Romans 3:10-17. He seems to sum it all up in verse 18: "There is no fear of God before their eyes." A low view of the holiness of God provides little restraint against sin. Contrariwise, a deep realization of the absolute holiness of God will not only uncover the corruption in the hearts of the best of men but will create a longing desire to be holy as God is holy (Isaiah 6:1-8).

*"For I am the Lord, I change not; therefore ye sons of Jacob are not consumed"* (3:6). Because of God's unchangeable, sovereign purpose for the nation of Israel, this nation will never be consumed as Edom was allowed to perish (1:3-4). He is the unchangeable God who keeps His covenants. The reason for Israel's promised survival and future

exaltation over all the gentile nations is in God alone. World empires of gentiles have perished: Babylon, Persia, Greece, Rome. But all promises in God's covenant relative to Israel will be fulfilled. The Messiah will sit upon the throne of David and with saved Israel will rule over the nations of the world (Luke 1:31-35, Revelation 19:15-16). Because of God's unchangeable covenant with Israel, all satanic efforts to destroy this nation must fail. Even in Israel's unsaved condition as a nation, it is under the unchangeable covenant of God and is being preserved even in times of terrible suffering. "Thus saith the Lord, who giveth the sun for a light by day and the ordinances of the moon and the stars for a light by night, who divideth the sea when its waves roar; the Lord of hosts is his name: If those ordinances depart from before me, saith the Lord, then the seed of Israel also shall cease from being a nation before me forever. Thus saith the Lord, If heaven above can be measured, and the foundations of the earth searched out beneath, I will also cast off all the seed of Israel for all that they have done, saith the Lord" (Jeremiah 31:35-37). God here states some extremely impossible things — things which cannot occur — to illustrate that it is impossible for the nation of Israel to ultimately cease.

A very interesting statement is found in Deuteronomy 8:17-18. Here God instructs Israel not to become proud and haughty when becoming prosperous. It is *God* who gives our Jewish friends the power to become prosperous. And hence His injunction: "But thou shalt remember the Lord thy God; for it is he who giveth thee power to get wealth, that he may establish his covenant which he swore unto thy fathers, as it is this day." Jewish proficiency in business, the professions, sciences, etc., is all part of God's provision to insure the survival of the nation, that He might keep His covenant with them.

There *is* a God of justice who is exercising universal judgment according to His holy and sovereign will!

**Chapter 8**

# *How Have We Robbed Thee?*

*"But ye say, How have we robbed thee?"* (3:8).

The priests had utterly failed to practice and to teach scriptural stewardship. This failure caused the curses of God to come upon the nation to whom they ministered.

It is worth noting that the Father, Son and Holy Spirit are each revealed in Scripture as deeply concerned with the giving habits of God's people.

God beholds the tithes and offerings of His people (3:8-9).

The Lord Jesus Christ watched the gifts in the temple (Luke 21:1-4).

The Holy Spirit was conscious of being lied to about Ananias' gift (Acts 5:1-3).

The purpose of giving is not entirely that God's work might prosper, but that God may be enabled to pour out great blessings upon His people. How this should speak to the Christian's heart.

There was clear evidence of greediness in the lives of the priests and people, for Malachi saw them reserving the best of the flock for themselves and offering the worthless to the Lord. Haggai mentioned the concern of the people in general for their own homes while neglecting to build a house for the living God to dwell among them (Haggai 1:2-5). Greediness also extended to the well-to-do who oppressed their brethren with crushing interest rates, for Nehemiah wrote: "I rebuked the nobles, and the rulers, and said unto them, Ye exact interest, everyone of his brother. And I held a great assembly against them" (Nehemiah 5:7). May not these failures at least in part be traced to the rebellious priests, who not only failed to *teach* proper unselfish giving but who also themselves did not *set an example* before the people by joyfully presenting tithes and offerings to the Lord?

How fitting the words of Isaiah to describe the self-seeking leaders and priests: "Yea, they are greedy dogs that can never have enough, and they are shepherds that cannot understand; they all look to their own way, every one for his gain" (Isaiah 56:11). "Woe be to the shepherds of Israel that do feed themselves! Should not the shepherd feed the flocks?" (Ezekiel 34:2).

This selfish neglect of bringing tithes and offerings to the Lord was of long standing. *"Even from the days of your fathers ye are gone away from mine ordinances, and have not kept them"* (3:7). God calls for His people to return unto Him. God had not overlooked this sin because of the passage of time. It is also to be noted that a long time of neglect in the past was no barrier to returning to

God now. *"Return unto me, and I will return unto you, saith the Lord of hosts"* (3:7). I will return to you with abundant blessings, long withheld because of your disobedience. What God commands, He also enables. When He calls upon people to turn, He will enable them to turn. "Turn us, O God of our salvation, and cause thine anger toward us to cease" (Psalm 85:4, KJV) should have been an appropriate prayer.

*"But ye said, In what way shall we return?"* (3:7) Is this an honest inquiry, or does it imply that they did not need to return because they had never been away from the Lord?

God immediately in great faithfulness points out the point of departure from Him by asking a question and stating the answer: *"Will a man rob God? Yet ye have robbed me"* (3:8). Frail creatures of time robbing the eternal God! This question and declaration should have startled the priests and the people into heart searching and repentance. Instead we have the rather defiant question, *"How have we robbed thee?"* God answers, *"In tithes and offerings."* This brings before us several basic truths of Scripture which should be thoroughly understood by all of God's people.

God, the Creator of the universe and all it contains, is therefore the owner of all wealth. "The earth is the Lord's, and the fullness thereof" (Psalm 24:1). "For every beast of the forest is mine, and the cattle upon a thousand hills" (Psalm 50:10). "The silver is mine, and the gold is mine, saith the Lord of hosts" (Haggai 2:8). The ability of Israel to acquire wealth is likewise from the Lord (Deuteronomy 8:17-18). We are but temporary custodians who someday must give account of our stewardship. "For we brought nothing into this world, and it is certain we can carry nothing out" (I Timothy 6:7). When we have the great opportunity of presenting our tithes and offerings to the Lord, we are giving Him what has always been His. David prayed, "But who am I, and what are my people, that we should be able to offer so willingly after this sort? For all things come of thee, and of thine own have we given thee" (I Chronicles 29:14). Nebuchadnezzar's proud boast that he himself was the origin of all his material prosperity was rebuked when God caused Nebuchadnezzar to be insane until he had learned his lesson (Daniel 4:28-37).

Now regarding tithes and offerings. Early in the Scriptures, Abram gave tithes to Melchizedek (Genesis 14:20). Levi, and in effect the entire priesthood, are seen as likewise paying *their* tithes when Abraham paid tithes to Melchizedek. "And as I may so say, Levi also, who received tithes, paid tithes in Abraham. For he was yet in the loins of his father when Melchizedek met him" (Hebrews 7:9-10). How important, therefore, for the present Levitical priesthood to pay tithes and to teach the people to tithe. Tithing in due time became part of the law and an act of worship (Leviticus 27:30, Deuteronomy 12:6, Numbers 18:26). Our Lord Jesus Christ spoke of the tithing of mint, anise and cummin as "these ought ye to have done," while also not omitting "the weightier matter of the law, justice, mercy and faith" (Matthew 23:23).

As to the present dispensation of grace, it is well to see the work of the Spirit of God in instructing the infant church relative to giving. "Neither said any of them that any of the things which he possessed was his own" (Acts 4:32), acknowledging the supreme ownership of God of all material things for the welfare of the whole body of Christ.

The Corinthian church was instructed by the Apostle Paul as follows: "Upon the first day of the week let every one of you lay by him in store, as God hath prospered him, that there be no gatherings when I come" (I Corinthians 16:2). The church at Corinth failed in the matter of giving, and it was necessary not only for Paul to write at length again regarding this great duty and privilege, but he also felt it necessary to send Titus to the church for the specific task of teaching the Corinthians the grace of giving (II Corinthians 8:1-9:15).

*"Ye are cursed with a curse; for ye have robbed me, even this whole nation"* (3:9). The priests brought this curse upon the nation because of their failure to practice and to teach the duty and privilege of presenting tithes and offerings unto the Lord. No man can rob God and prosper. The curses for disobedience are enumerated in Deuteronomy 28:15-68. Seven times in this short book of Malachi does God mention an impending curse upon the disobedient priesthood and people. If

the Israelites robbed God of their tithes and offerings, the nation was at the same time robbing themselves of God's abundant blessing. We must open our little treasures for God before He can make available His vast wealth for us.

*"Bring ye all the tithes into the storehouse"* (3:10). This is a command requiring voluntary action. The results of such obedience are manifold. There will be sufficient funds to carry on the work of the temple, God will be proven true, and He will open the windows of heaven and pour out such a blessing that there will not be room enough to receive it.

Agricultural judgments — necessary because of disobedience in failing to tithe — will end when Israel, repentant, is once more obedient to God (Joel 1:4, Haggai 1:6). *"And I will rebuke the devourer for your sakes, and he shall not destroy the fruits of your ground; neither shall your vine cast its fruit before the time in the field"* (3:11). Israel will also again be a testimony to the nations, as was promised to Abraham. *"And all nations shall call you blessed; for ye shall be a delightsome land, saith the Lord of hosts"* (3:12).

How frightful Israel's answer to this plea of God. Instead of acknowledging failure and turning to God in contrition and repentance, their words are still stout (arrogant) against God, questioning His promise of blessing to all who serve Him (3:13). Answering them, God tells them what they said: *"It is vain to serve God; and what profit is it*

## HOW HAVE WE ROBBED THEE?

*that we have kept his ordinance?"* (3:14). Israel thus disputed God's statement about abundant *"blessing, that there shall not be room enough to receive it"* (3:10).

Yet Israel claims that they have kept God's law! What about the defiled, second-rate offerings? What about the divorces and the ungodly marriages to unbelievers? What about the failure to pay tithes and offerings? In all these ways the people *had cheated their God!* How could Israel say they had kept His ordinances? What blindness and self-deception!

The claim also is made that *"we have walked mournfully before the Lord of hosts"* (3:14). It is difficult to find any evidence of this. Perhaps it was "ashes on the forehead and not in the heart." The words of Isaiah 58:3-7, being words that go into detail about pretended mourning and fasting without an amended life, are surely appropriate.

These arrogant disputers with God were also questioning His justice. Hence their topsy-turvy words: *"And now we call the proud happy; yea, they that work wickedness are set up; yea, they that test God are even delivered"* (3:15). These words of gross spiritual confusion are a restatement of the complaint recorded earlier: "Every one that doeth evil is good in the sight of the Lord, and he delighteth in them" (2:17). The cry "Where is the God of justice?" was again being raised. Had they not grasped the Lord's answer given through Malachi earlier in this chapter (3:1-6)? Evidently not. Have we? As we view the obvious and blatant injustices in our present time, have we, with the additional revelation we have received, been willing to see God's hand of power and grace as still in control and bringing to pass the outworking of His divine plan? And have we yielded ourselves to Him as agents in the spreading of His righteousness? Or have we been robbing God of His due allegiance? Do we live with "the pride of life" (I John 2:16) in control, and as if we could put God to the test and escape? Or have we hearkened to His gracious words, "Return unto me, and I will return unto you"?

What is God's plan for blessing His work today? It is for the pastor to practice biblical stewardship himself first. It is well that he begin with a tithe of all income, but not to stop there. As God so abundantly blesses, the pastor will be led joyfully to go way beyond the tithe. Constantly he will find God far outgiving him. Then the pastor is to patiently and lovingly share with the people what he has learned about the teaching of Scripture and the blessing that has come to his own life through proper stewardship.

God's people are to support God's work. It is best to eliminate all financial gimmicks and pleas to the unsaved — such as inviting an ungodly neighborhood to come to a church supper, raffle, rummage sale, bazaar or cake sale to finance the Lord's work. Reach out to your neighborhood —yes! But not in this way or for this purpose. "*My*

*God* shall supply all your needs" (Philippians 4:19). But this promise does not apply to all churches or to all Christians. It applied to the Philippians because of their excellent stewardship (Philippians 4:10-17), and it *can* apply to *us!* This text is also true: "But this I say, He who soweth sparingly shall reap also sparingly; and he who soweth bountifully shall reap also bountifully" (II Corinthians 9:6).

It was quite evident that the great needs of the people of Malachi's time were not being met; instead, curses were threatened because of their failure to bring tithes and offerings to God. What is the situation with us?

May the pastor and the leaders of each church assume the responsibility of practicing and teaching biblical stewardship — not just of material possessions, but of spiritual gifts and time and talents. For experience has convincingly demonstrated that the church which teaches and practices total Christian stewardship enjoys *abundant spiritual blessings* as well as *all material needs well met.*

## Chapter 9

# *The Precious God-Fearers*

*"Then they that feared the Lord spoke often one to another"* (3:16).

In every time of spiritual decline God will raise up unto Himself a group, generally small, of God-fearers. Quite often these people have separated from a larger group which has departed from the Word of God even though they are still performing the motions of ministry. God honors this little flock with His presence as they labor to preserve the truth of God. These God-fearers have the mind of God in spiritual discernment and hence the needed message of God for their time.

Despite the pervasive departure from the Word of God by the priests and their misguided followers, there remained, in Malachi's day, such a group of faithful ones. This little band did not use the decay of the priesthood as an excuse for coldness and lack of interest in the things of God. Nor should we. There is no time so dark that earnest souls cannot enjoy heart-communion with the Lord. Enoch and Noah walked with God in the dark, perilous times which necessitated the judgment of the flood. Simeon and Anna were among the few who were living Spirit-filled lives in their time — a time of deep declension in Israel — and hence recognized the infant Jesus as the Son of God (Luke 2:25-38).

The hearts of those who feared the Lord were touched by the holiness of God and were drawn around Him, and so to each other. Unity around the person of Christ is the burden of the prayer of our Lord Jesus: "That they all may be one, as thou, Father, art in me, and I in thee, that they also may be one in us" (John 17:21). How far above mere outward organizational unity this is, even as desirable as organizational unity may be. However, the Ecumenical Movement, which is attempting to unite all professing Christians into one organization, a world church, can never have the full blessing of God, for such lowest-common-denominator unity today necessitates compromising the precious Word of God.

Apparently this group of God-fearers was neither large nor prominent. They were ignored by the religious leaders and their followers, but honored by the Lord. *He* knew exactly who they were.

We are told that *"they . . . spoke often one to another"* (3:16). What they said to each other flowed out of heart-devotion to the Lord. What a holy joy it was to be with those of like precious faith! "They that fear thee will be glad when they see me, because I have hoped in thy word" (Psalm 119:74). "Come and hear, all ye that fear God, and

# THE PRECIOUS GOD-FEARERS

I will declare what he hath done for my soul" (Psalm 66:16).

This group met often, feeling a constant need to strengthen each other in a time of ungodly leadership. Those who reverence God's name usually are drawn to each other — they find each other.

The result of their fellowshiping together was that *"the Lord hearkened and heard"* (3:16). "For where two or three are gathered together in my name, there am I in the midst of them" (Matthew 18:20). The Lord drew near to listen to their communing; just as later, after His resurrection, Jesus drew near to two sorrowing, bewildered believers (Luke 24:13-32). Bewildered hearts were changed into burning hearts by His presence.

*"And a book of remembrance was written before him"* (3:16). Our Lord caused a book to be written and to be placed before Him. It seems that this book was to record great exploits, afterward to be remembered with suitable rewards.

Mordecai, by exposing a plot, had saved the life of King Ahasuerus. This noble deed "was written in the book of the chronicles before the king" (Esther 2:21-23). In the gracious providence of God, the king had a sleepless night and called for this book, the record of his reign, to be read before him. He asked, "What honor and dignity hath been bestowed upon Mordecai for this?" The king's attendant answered, "There has nothing been done for him" (Esther 6:1-3). And soon afterward Mordecai was wonderfully honored.

Is it not a precious truth that when God-fearers meet to honor and to think upon His name, God records this as a great exploit worthy of reward?

This little group *"feared the Lord, and thought upon his name"* (3:16). How wonderful to meditate together upon His holiness, His power, His love, and all His glorious attributes. This personal knowledge of the Lord was apparently shared as each expressed a desire for holiness and guidance in life and ministry.

Is this not a clear indication of what God's people should be doing in an ungodly age? God was their exceeding joy and their reward.

It is such a joy to find pastors and Christian workers whose main concern is fellowship with the living Christ. It is a shame that so often, rather, our conversations concern mainly programs, statistics, news items, etc. May we be like this treasured group, meditating upon the name of the Lord: God's "name-fearers."

*"And they shall be mine, saith the Lord of hosts, in that day when I make up my jewels"* (3:17). What a promise! These God-fearers will be publicly displayed as the Lord's own peculiar treasure. We sense His unspeakable tenderness as He acknowledges His "name-fearers" at the time when all ungodliness is judged (II Thessalonians 1:7-10).

"In that day..." — this day is mentioned in 4:1: "Behold, the day cometh that shall burn like an oven...." It speaks of the long day of God's final judgments. We are His treasure, even as He is our treasure. Paul speaks of "the riches of the glory of [God's] inheritance in the saints" (Ephesians 1:18). The believers are a "people of his own" (I Peter 2:9) — His unique treasure!

*"And I will spare them, as a man spareth his own son that serveth him"* (3:17). Spared from God's wrath, spared for God's blessing. "For God hath not appointed us to wrath but to obtain salvation by our Lord Jesus Christ" (I Thessalonians 5:9). God promises to exercise His fatherly love and care with abundant blessing upon the God-fearers, even "as a man spareth his own son that serveth him." Earthly fathers, who are evil, know how to give good gifts to their children; so how much more will a holy Father give unspeakable gifts to His obedient children (Matthew 7:11). The Father's love, power, wisdom and infinite resources wait to bless the obedient children. "Wherefore, come out from among them and be ye separate, saith the Lord, and touch not the unclean thing; and I will receive you, and will be a Father unto you, and ye shall be my sons and daughters, saith the Lord Almighty" (II Corinthians 6:17-18).

*"Then shall ye return, and discern between the righteous and the wicked, between him that serveth God and him that serveth him not"* (3:18). This verse speaks of spiritual discernment by God's people. It is the Holy Spirit who leads us into the deeper things of God and enables us to more and more understand the mind of God (I Corinthians 2:9-16). This discernment of the true and the false

should be an increasing possession of all of God's children now. However, when we are glorified and reigning with the Lord, this discernment will be greatly enlarged so that then the saints will be able to judge the world and even the rebellious, fallen angels (I Corinthians 6:2-3). It is of this time that this verse is specifically speaking.

How few among the priests and those whom the priests blindly led had spiritual discernment! What a need there is among God's people today to wait constantly upon the Lord so as to grow in spiritual discernment! How necessary to glorify God; how necessary to be a spiritual blessing to others! Only by spiritual discernment constantly learned in the presence of God can anyone make known the mind of God to those who are in need.

How precious to God are these God-fearers!

**Chapter 10**

# *The Terrible, Glorious Day of the Lord*

*"For, behold, the day cometh . . ."* (4:1).

Thank God for this wonderful assurance! There will be a glorious, righteous consummation of all things. The world is not like a car without a driver, plunging down a precipice out of control. "Then cometh the end, when he shall have delivered up the kingdom to God, even the Father, when he shall have put down all rule and all authority and power. For he must reign till he hath put all enemies under his feet.... And when all things shall be subdued unto him, then shall the Son also himself be subject unto him that put all things under him, that God may be all in all" (I Corinthians 15:24-25, 28). This wonderful "Day of the Lord" begins with the translation of the church to be with the Lord and concludes with a new heaven and a new earth and a new Jerusalem, the holy city. How wonderful eternity will be! God has already written the last chapter of all things. He is in control.

What comfort to look away from the present time of satanic world power, which is bringing upon the earth "distress of nations, with perplexity ['having no way out' — Greek], . . . men's hearts failing them for fear" (Luke 21:25-26). The threat of nuclear war with its unthinkably horrible consequences hangs over the world. In such times as these, we have comforting and assuring words from the One under whose feet all shall bow someday in complete submission: "And ye shall hear of wars and rumors of wars; see that ye be not troubled" (Matthew 24:6).

The troubles of the world are not to get into the heart of the believer. He is, of course, to work and pray for peace and for those in authority (I Timothy 2:1-3). However, the informed believer sees no permanent hope for this world apart from the coming of the Day of the Lord. If the Christian worker does not follow the command of Christ to live untroubled in a troubled world, he will have no victory in Christ to declare to others.

*"For, behold, the day cometh, that shall burn like an oven"* (4:1). The intense white heat of an oven is a graphic portrayal of the wrath of God. Our Lord's very presence in judgment is as a fire. "For our God is a consuming fire" (Hebrews 12:29). "His eyes were like a flame of fire" (Revelation 1:14). "And to you who are troubled, rest with us, when the Lord Jesus shall be revealed from heaven with his mighty angels, in flaming fire taking vengeance on them that know not God, and that obey not the gospel of our Lord Jesus Christ; who shall be punished with everlasting destruction

from the presence of the Lord, and from the glory of his power" (II Thessalonians 1:7-9). "He will burn up the chaff with unquenchable fire" (Matthew 3:12).

*"All the proud, yea, and all that do wickedly, shall be stubble; and the day that cometh shall burn them up, saith the Lord of hosts, that it shall leave them neither root nor branch"* (4:1). Pride, the first sin of the universe (Isaiah 14:12-14), is still the basic sin of man. Fallen man at heart is still a rebel against God, always putting his rebellious will first. "We have turned every one to his own way" (Isaiah 53:6). The Day of the Lord with its righteous fire of judgment will bring to an end forever all rebellion against God. All the vain boasts of proud men will be seen in that day as mere stubble, and the proud will be destroyed, both "root and branch." Jesus declared: "Every plant which my heavenly Father hath not planted shall be rooted up" (Matthew 15:13).

While on a visit to Syria years ago, I observed a farmer letting the wind separate the wheat from the chaff. As the wheat was hurled into the wind, the grain fell near his feet while the worthless chaff whirled about his face. Sometime later I came upon these searching words: "Am I the wheat which falls in full surrender at my Lord's feet, or am I the chaff which flies in His face in rebellion?"

The next word, "but," introduces a tremendous contrast — what this day will mean to the godly "name-fearers." *"But unto you that fear my name shall the Sun of righteousness arise with healing in his wings*" (4:2). What a time of glorious healing it will be for us who have been redeemed by the blood of Christ! The saints will be forever healed, with glorified bodies and spirits made perfect (Philippians 3:20-21, Hebrews 12:23)! Israel as a nation will be saved (Romans 11:26)! The nations, too, will be healed (Revelation 22:1-2)! *All* creation will be healed (II Peter 3:10-14)! Eternal healing!

"*And ye* [the 'name-fearers'] *shall go forth, and grow up like calves of the stall*" (4:2). This verse seems to imply that like cattle cramped in confining stalls during the night go forth at sunrise as from a prison house, so the saints with the new freedom of eternity will leap with eternal life when the Sun of righteousness appears.

"*And ye shall tread down the wicked; for they shall be ashes under the soles of your feet in the day that I shall do this, saith the Lord of hosts*" (4:3). The "name-fearers" in that day gladly put their feet where the feet of their victorious, glorious Lord are — with all enemies under His feet. All these wicked ones are likewise subdued under the feet of the redeemed!

"*Behold, I will send you Elijah the prophet, before the coming of the great and terrible day of the Lord*" (4:5). Here is a clear prophecy that Elijah, who has been in Glory since his miraculous translation (II Kings 2:11), will come back to earth again to have a special ministry to the world and to the people of God *before* the "great and terrible" aspect of the Day of the Lord. John the Baptist ministered in the spirit of Elijah, but was not Elijah, for "they asked him, What then? Art thou Elijah? And he [John the Baptist] saith, I am not" (John 1:21).

There are two witnesses of the Lord mentioned in Revelation 11:3-13. "These have power to shut heaven, that it rain not in the days of their prophecy" (vs. 6). This clearly seems to be a reference to the similar ministry of Elijah in the days of the reign of wicked King Ahab: "And Elijah, the Tishbite, who was of the inhabitants of Gilead, said unto Ahab, As the Lord God of Israel liveth, before whom I stand, there shall not be dew nor rain these years but according to my word" (I Kings 17:1). Elijah's companion witness is possibly Moses. If so, this would help to explain the seemingly out-of-place charge to *"Remember the law of Moses, my servant, which I commanded unto him in Horeb for all Israel, with the statutes and ordinances,"* found in verse 4 of this chapter in Malachi. As disobedience to God's precepts brought distress in Elijah's day, so in the time of these two witnesses. "And they shall prophesy a thousand two hundred and threescore days, clothed in sackcloth" (vs. 3).

One cannot help but wonder what an appropriate message in such a time as that should include. Certainly it would have to be a fearless, unpopular message. How wonderful was the fearless, sacrificial life of Elijah while on earth, as he single-handedly faced and defeated all the prophets of Baal on Mt. Carmel. That surely has prepared him for this future ministry requiring such supernatural fearlessness and courage. It will be a time when the Christ-rejecting world will be worshiping the Beast. The harlot church will be using the Beast to extend her worldwide spiritual fornication. A treaty entered into by Israel with the Beast will prove to be a tragic disaster. So to preach against these and other errors and to declare that the Lord Jesus Christ is soon to return in glory would seem to be at least part of the necessary message of Elijah. No wonder the message will be so unpopular that it results in his and his companion's assassination in Jerusalem by the Beast.

The ungodly on earth will rejoice over the murder of these two faithful witnesses, and endeavor to disgrace them further by putting the dead bodies on exhibition. "And they of the peoples and kindreds and tongues and nations shall see their dead bodies three days and a half, and shall not permit their dead bodies to be put in graves" (vs. 9). Great celebration breaks out all over the ungodly world, with people having parties and exchanging gifts in celebration. Then suddenly — like the horror at Belshazzar's ungodly feast when the supernatural handwriting of God appeared on the wall of his palace, indicating the soon fall of his empire — great fear falls upon the previously careless, celebrating populace. "The spirit of life from God entered into them, and they stood upon their feet, and great fear fell upon them who saw them" (vs. 11). God thus vindicates His messengers and their message. Judgment is coming! "And they heard a great voice from heaven saying unto them, Come up here. And they ascended up to heaven in a cloud, and their enemies beheld them" (vs. 12). God will give further witness that judgment is ahead by sending an earthquake, because of which a tenth part of the city falls and seven thousand perish. How quickly God can change things! In the meanwhile, the little godly remnant, perhaps often in fearful seclusion, are filled with awe and give glory to the God of heaven (vs. 13).

The purpose of Elijah's ministry in that day will be to *"turn the heart of the fathers to the children, and the heart of the children to their fathers"* (4:6). The shame which the fathers feel regarding their children, and which the children feel toward their fathers — because of the absence of a common bond of union in Christ — will be removed. Elijah's ministry in the past was also designed to turn back the unbelieving children of the generation to whom he ministered to the faith of their believing ancestors, Abraham, Isaac, Jacob and others.

If Elijah's ministry does not accomplish this renewal for these multitudes, then for them the coming of the Messiah will be a curse and not a blessing. *". . . lest I come and smite the earth with a curse"* (4:6). It will be the curse of the broken law; the curse of having rejected God and His gracious offer of salvation. "Cursed is everyone that continueth not in all things which are written in the book of the law, to do them" (Galatians 3:10). How wonderful for all who put their faith in the Lord Jesus Christ that "Christ hath redeemed us from the curse of the law, being made a curse for us" (Galatians 3:13). Praise His matchless name!

**Chapter 11**

# *Conclusion*

Thus this short, inspired book of Malachi ends. What spiritual principles are here for all pastors and Christian workers! The pitfalls to certain disaster are clearly pointed out. Likewise the pathway to a Spirit-filled, fruitful, God-glorifying life is also clearly set before God's servants.

Is not the secret of all fruitful ministry daily, unbroken heart-communion with the Lord Jesus Christ? Anything less is cheating God and oneself. The knowledge of Christ is to be sought as the one great purpose of life. From this fellowship with Christ all fruitful ministry will flow. "Out of his heart shall flow rivers of living water" is our Savior's promise (John 7:38).

It is so easy for the Christian to gradually become more and more devoted to the *interests of Christ* rather than to Christ Himself. This is a perilous situation which can only lead to loss of testimony and to fruitlessness.

Let us prayerfully meditate on the testimony of

Christ concerning the church at Ephesus (Revelation 2:1-7). It was a working church. It was twice commended by our Lord for its patience. It could not tolerate sin or apostasy and was defending the name of Christ. It had endurance, with no thought of turning back. However, this church was in a fallen condition and about to lose its light — its testimony. "Remember, therefore, from where thou art fallen, and repent and do the first works, or else I will come unto thee quickly and remove thy lampstand out of its place, except thou repent" (vs. 5). The church had perhaps slowly but surely moved away from heart-devotion to Christ. "Thou hast left thy first love" (vs. 4). It could be said of this church that it never wavered in its fundamentalism . . . but it dried up in its vital experience of heart-communion with the Lord Jesus Christ.

Would it do violence to I Corinthians 13 to enlarge as follows? Though I am thoroughly conversant with Hebrew, Aramaic, Arabic, Ugaritic and Greek, and though I understand all the mysteries of sacred Scripture so that I am able to harmonize God's sovereignty and man's responsibility, and though I understand all prophecies including those in Daniel, Zechariah and Revelation, and though I have great faith and also live a sacrificial life concerning material possessions, and am willing to lay down my life, . . . if I do not exercise all these gifts in love, out of heart-devotion to Christ, as far as fruit is concerned *it is all worthless.*

Some years ago the writer was in a very serious

condition spiritually. Though I had served in the pastorate for about fifteen years, my work for God had become a barren weariness. Was the victorious, fruitful life for just a few chosen vessels like George Muller, Andrew Murray, F. B. Meyer and Hudson Taylor? Or was this life of victorious fruitfulness provided for all God's servants? So, up went a desperate cry to God. He graciously answered by directing me to meditate upon the scriptures concerning the church at Ephesus. Day after day this passage was studied and prayed over. Gradually a marvelous change took place. *Christ now became the center!* My whole life is now lived in joyous, fruitful heart-communion with Him. How wonderful He has been, despite all human weaknesses and failures.

Our Lord's extremely significant question to Peter, as Peter was commissioned to feed His lambs and tend His sheep, was: "Peter, do you love me?" (John 21:15).

> We love to spread our branches;
> The root of life we neglect.
> We love to shine in public
> And human praise expect.
> While in the hidden Temple
> Where creature voices cease,
> We may meet God in silence
> And drink in heaven's peace.
>      — Max Isaac Reich

## *Biographical Sketch*

Pastor Newton C. Conant was born on November 18, 1900. His formal theological training was at Faith Theological Seminary, Wilmington, Delaware. He was pastor of the Calvary Methodist Protestant Church, Camden, N.J. (later changed to Bible Protestant) for approximately forty years. In September 1939, he was called to lead out from the proposed union of all Methodism a group of thirty-four churches who refused to enter the union because of serious doctrinal differences. He became the first president of the newly formed denomination, The Bible Protestant Church. In 1971, at the age of seventy, he was called of God to go to Africa as a missionary. He taught in the Ukamba Bible School and in Scott Theological College, Kenya. His ministry was also to missionaries in Kenya, Uganda, Zaire and Tanzania. Returning in 1975, he became chaplain of the Harvey Cedars (New Jersey) Bible Conference. In 1976 he became interim pastor of Easton Union Church, Mt. Holly, N.J. In September 1977, he became pastor of the Cinnaminson Baptist church, Cinnaminson, N.J., serving until June, 1982. He is at present chaplain at Biblical Seminary, Hatfield, Pennsylvania. He is the author of the following books:

*Present-Day Methodism and the Bible*
*How God Delivered 34 Churches*
*Changed by Beholding Him*

He is presently residing at Rydal Park Apartments, Apt. 452, Rydal, Pennsylvania 19046.